25
QUESTIONS
FOR A
JEWISH
MOTHER

25 QUESTIONS FOR A JEWISH MOTHER

Judy Gold
and
Kate Moira Ryan

VOICE

Hyperion • New York

Library of Congress Cataloging-in-Publication Data

Gold, Judy
    25 questions for a Jewish mother / Judy Gold and Kate Moira Ryan. — 1st ed.
        p. cm.
    ISBN-13: 978-1-4013-0311-2
    ISBN-10: 1-4013-0311-0
    1. Gold, Judy. 2. Comedians—United States—Biography. 3. Jewish women—
United States—Interviews. 4. Mothers—United States—Interviews. I. Ryan, Kate
Moira. II. Title. III. Title: Twenty five questions for a Jewish mother.
    PN2287.G575A3 2007
    792.702'8092—dc22
    [B]

                                                          2007000630

Hyperion books are available for special promotions and premiums.
For details contact Michael Rentas, Assistant Director,
Inventory Operations, Hyperion, 77 West 66th Street,
12th floor, New York, New York 10023, or call 212-456-0133.

Design by Jo Anne Metsch
Illustrations by Harry Bliss

FIRST EDITION

10 9 8 7 6 5 4 3 2 1

CONTENTS

Contents

ACKNOWLEDGMENTS

WE'D LIKE TO THANK PAM DORMAN, ELLEN ARCHER, SARAH Landis, and Kathleen Carr for their patience and care in guiding us through this book. We are incredibly excited to be part of VOICE in its inaugural imprint. We are indebted to our wonderful agent and Kate's partner, Laurie Liss at Sterling Lord. We'd also like to thank Beth Blickers at Abrams Artists, Rick Dorfman at Relevant Entertainment, and Conan Smith at Endeavor for their unflagging support of this project through these past six years. They gave us encouragement when no one else would. We are truly blessed to have these three in our lives.

Our director, Karen Kohlhaas, and our amazing design team, Jorge Muelle, Louisa Thompson, and Jennifer Tipton, put together a production that we could only envision in our wildest dreams. The play would not have happened without our incredible producing team at Ars Nova: Jason Eagan, Jon Steingart, Jenny Weiner, and their wonderful staff, Teresa Bass, Jillian Apfelbaum, and Richard Di Bella. We cannot express our appreciation enough to Alan Kanoff (co-producer) for still showing up at least once a week, Chris Mazilli, Tara Fishman, and our tireless stage manager, Damon Arrington. We could not have done this project without the support of Robin Kampf, Naomi Newman, and Jodi Lieberman at the Montreal Comedy Festival. Thank you to Joan Smith, Marjorie and Sy Cohen, Lisa Troland, Mike Berkowitz, and Allison Narver at the Empty Space Theatre (for giving us our first shot).

A special thank-you to all the women we interviewed.

And a very, very special thanks to our children, Henry and Benjamin Callahan-Gold, and Timothy Ryan-Liss.

25

QUESTIONS
FOR A
JEWISH
MOTHER

JUDY: AS A COMEDIAN, I OFTEN HAVE BEEN CRITICIZED FOR promoting stereotypes of Jewish women—especially Jewish mothers. (I've always contended that they really don't need any help from me.) One particular reporter from the *Jewish Daily Forward* called my manager repeatedly to complain after I appeared on *The Tonight Show*. I had done my Anne Frank joke—which is a signature bit of mine. In the joke I try to imagine my family living silently in that small space the Franks occupied. I don't think there would be any way we would have survived a single weekend, let alone two years. I'm sure if we were in that situation, it would have gone something like this:

"JUDITH! I asked you to wash that dish ten minutes ago!"

(sotto voce) "Ma, shut-up we're all going to get caught."

"That's right, we're all going to get caught, because

you couldn't wash a G-d damn dish! (Pause) Great. They're here. They're knocking. You proud of yourself?"

That same reporter confronted me at a benefit I did for the Anti-Defamation League. She walked up to me and said, "Ms. Gold, when are you going to leave Jewish mothers alone?" And I said, "Will you give it up? I'm a practicing Jew and I am a mother." Her steno book dropped to the floor, and she said in a tone that was either hostile or incredulous—actually probably a mixture of both—"You are?" And I thought, You know, she's right. I am not the typical Jewish mother I make fun of in my act. I've always wanted to be the "young and fun" kind of mom and not some secondary character in a Philip Roth novel. For most of my adult life, I have struggled with the conflicts of being Jewish as well as being gay, and being a comedian as well as a mother. Honestly, what Jewish mother do you know who spends her evenings in smoky clubs full of drunk people, shouting obscenities over the sound of a blender, and the next day drops her kids off at Hebrew school?

I am a six-foot-three kosher stand-up comedian bringing up two kids on the Upper West Side of Manhattan with my former partner Wendy. I have a ten-year-old named Henry to whom Wendy gave birth, and a five-year-old named Ben to whom I gave birth. I'm like a documentary premiering at a gay film festival in Berlin, *Das Orthodyke*. So when my friend Kate, who's also a playwright, suggested we examine how and where I fit into the world of Jewish motherhood, I jumped at the chance to see if there were any other Jewish mothers out there like me, or if they were all, G-d forbid, like my mother. Unbeknownst to us, Kate and I embarked on what would become a five-year odyssey across America, armed with just a tape recorder, sometimes a video camera, and a list of twenty-five questions.

When we first started this project, I told my friend and producer at HBO, Naomi Newman, about it, and she immediately wanted to be involved, so she set up our first sets of interviews. Coming from an Orthodox background, she had a good time rounding up all her mother's friends. We ended each set of interviews by asking, "Do you know any other women we should speak to?"

We always left each house with a handful of rugelach wrapped in a napkin and a batch of new phone numbers. We never knew where or to whom those phone numbers would lead. The only requirement we had was that they be mothers and Jewish. Sometimes we changed a pronoun or the length was edited, but we never rewrote what the women said to make it more dramatic. The hardest thing for us was deciding which monologues to use. We knew we couldn't include them all, so we picked the ones that related directly to my own journey. I'd like to thank all of these women for opening their homes to us and sharing their lives. I've always said that every woman has a story to tell, and how I created a play about Jewish mothers with an Irish Catholic woman named Kate Moira Ryan is a story in itself.

———————

Kate: It wasn't until a *New York Post* writer dubbed me "the improbably named Kate Moira Ryan" that I realized how weird it was for some people that I collaborated on this project with Judy. I blame Liz Smith and Grey Goose vodka. My partner (a literary agent) had dragged me along to BEA, the national booksellers' convention, in Chicago in 2000. I begged her to finagle an invite to a party for Liz Smith's new book, *Natural Blonde* (which, FYI, is a great book). As a Catholic school girl with falling down kneesocks, I had grown up reading her gossip column. I was constantly reading the *New York Post* and worrying to my mother over the state of Truman Capote's health: "I think if he keeps partying like that, he'll never publish again."

"Kathleen, Sister Constance called—did you turn in a book report on *Rubyfruit Jungle*?"

I held up the *Post*.

"Mom, look how wan Truman looks. I heard he had a falling out with Babe Paley."

"Kathleen, just hand in what she wants, okay? One more call from that harridan and I am canceling *The New Yorker*."

After two days of begging, Laurie procured the invitations

to Liz Smith's book party, and I was ecstatic. She had also gotten an extra ticket for Judy Gold. (We had met in Provincetown about five summers before and immediately hit it off.) I tracked down Judy, and we arranged to hook up at the party, where there were Grey Goose martinis the size of tiny buckets. After one, I was transported back into the world of the seventies, complete with swirling disco lights. My witty (however imaginary) chat with Fran Lebowitz screeched to a halt when six-foot-three-inch Judy loomed over me and shouted, "Listen, Kate, you have to get me out of the clubs. I'm sick of the clubs. If you don't get me out of the clubs, I'm going to kill myself."

By now I had known Judy for a while, and she had never once sounded so desperate. "I can't raise a kid on the road. I can't." I don't know if it was the Grey Goose or just being in the magic aura of Liz Smith, but I said, "Why don't I write a one-person show with you?" Much to my surprise and then fear, Judy agreed.

"Okay, but what's it going to be about? I wasn't molested as a child, and I don't have an eating disorder—well, I do, but not the kind that's useful and going to keep me skinny."

I speared an alcohol-soaked olive and replied, "Let's do it about Jewish mothers. We'll go around the country and interview Jewish mothers and see how you fit into the spectrum."

Judy got excited. "But what would we ask them?"

I grabbed a napkin and a pen.

During that alcohol-soaked night, we came up with a list of twenty-five questions on the back of that napkin. I often remind Judy of that night. Were we insane? Yes, I was a playwright, but I had never written a one-person show. I knew she was funny, had seen her stand-up a hundred times, but I didn't even know if she could act. After we left Liz's party and poured ourselves into a cab, she said, "This is my dream."

It took five years of hard work to bring this dream to reality. It wasn't always easy; there were many times that I wanted to quit. A first, the women we were interviewing would take one look at me and say, "You. You're not Jewish, not with that nose."

It did not matter that my partner is Jewish and we're raising our son Jewish. I felt like the outsider I was. But, as time went on, I became as obsessed as Judy was with the project.

We approached the interviews from two different perspectives. She was interested in the emotional journeys of the women; I was interested in their family histories. The more we asked, the more they told us. I couldn't believe how much the women opened up. Something was happening to us as the interviews went on. I couldn't put a finger on why this project was so important until one evening, when an adult child of Holocaust survivors sat down and said, "I never wanted to know what happened to my parents. I did not want to imagine them without hair, without teeth. Then my father died. His story was gone. My husband said, 'You have to ask your mother what happened. We should have it for the girls. They will want to know.' But I did not want to ask. So he hired a court reporter who sat with my mother for two days and transcribed her story. I sat outside the door and wondered, What, what is she saying? Her story was typed up and given to my husband in a folder. It lay on the dining room table. I looked at it every day and finally said to my husband, 'Get it out of my sight.' He rented a safe deposit box and put my mother's story in it. I have the key. Maybe one day."

For days I thought of that woman. How many of these women's stories were locked up? How many years had they waited to share what they knew, what they felt? Then I realized it did not matter if an Irish Catholic from Yonkers was working on a project about Jewish mothers. What mattered was that these stories were being told and that people listen.

We never asked the twenty-five questions in the same order. But, no matter how much we jumped around, we always started each interview with the same question. "What makes a Jewish mother different from a non-Jewish mother?"

#1

What makes a Jewish mother different from a non-Jewish mother?

"Jewish mothers love their children more."

ONE ORTHODOX WOMAN IN HER sixties shouted this with such force at Kate that her blond pageboy wig was knocked askew. I kicked Kate and whispered, "Told you so."

"Go to question number twenty-five, Jude," Kate shot back, rolling her eyes, effectively ending the interview.

For the most part when we asked this question, we received the answers that I termed the "chicken soup answers," like "Jewish mothers are different from non-Jewish mothers because of (a) the level of neurosis, (b) guilt (and guilt is not so bad), (c) the catchall, paranoia."

A thin dentist in her late forties from Arizona with two young children entered my apartment on the Upper West Side of Manhattan in the middle of the afternoon in late

October. She refused to take off her coat: "I was told that the interviews wouldn't take more than twenty minutes."

As Kate tried to get the woman to sit, I plied her with coffee, which she had initially refused. Quickly, her story tumbled out of her. She had grown up in America and spent part of her childhood in Israel and Germany. Perhaps because of the latter experiences, she gave what seemed a disproportionate amount of her income to the Jewish Defense League. When we started the interview and asked her question number one, she started to give us chicken soup answer (b). Then her voice faltered and she gripped her coffee mug filled with unwanted coffee and tried to meet our eyes. She was more nervous than shy, and I could see that she wanted to answer truthfully, but was scared of being judged. So I looked at her and said, "You're the only one in the room. Tell us what you really think."

She sighed and then took off her coat. Suddenly her demeanor changed and she took a sip of coffee and winced. (Okay, I like it strong.)

"Okay. This is going to sound silly. I mean we live in America. My children are Americans. But both my parents' families were all but decimated by the Holocaust. After they emigrated, my mother got a Christian neighbor to agree to hide her children if anything like what happened in Germany should happen here. And after I had my kids,

and even though it was so many years later, I asked one of my Christian neighbors the same thing. 'Would you hide my children if anything were to happen?' What makes me a Jewish mother is that sometimes I look at my children and I feel afraid."

"The hand-wringing angst."
(Mother of three, public relations executive, nonpracticing)

Is there something genetic in the Jewish mother DNA that separates her from the non-Jewish mother? Are Jewish mothers more paranoid? Is there some basis for the belief that everyone is out to get them? You know the first book my mother ever read to me as a child? It wasn't *Little Bear* or *The Cat in the Hat*. No, it was the pop-up version of *The Diary of Anne Frank*.

"I still believe that people are really good at heart. Now pull the tab, Judith. Alive. Pull it again. Dead."

"Most Jewish mothers are children-centered."
(Mother of four, homemaker, Orthodox)

I grew up in Clark, New Jersey, in a kosher observant home with my older siblings, Alan and Jane. My parents were both in their forties when they had me. My father served in Europe during World War II and married my mother soon after. My father thought that everyone was out to get the Jews, and my mother agreed. It was a perfect match. My father was a tax attorney, and my mother, in between B'nai B'rith and bridge, kept track of her three kids every hour, every minute, every second of every day. Once I was forty-five minutes late for dinner, and when I arrived home I noticed a police car in the driveway. I walked in and there was my mother, waving my school picture and serving the police rugelach, saying, "No, she's not eighteen, she's seven. She's just tall for her age."

After the police left, all hell broke loose. My mother picked up the phone and said, "Hello, is this the really scary, really abusive reform school featured on *Channel Seven News* last night? I was wondering if you have any openings for a tall little girl who doesn't listen to her mother? No? Okay, thanks anyway. Please put us on the waiting list. So long."

The next day my mother attached an egg timer to my belt when I went out to play, and when the bell went off, that was my signal to go home. I could never play hide-and-seek with my friends because no matter how quiet I was there was always this ticking sound to give me away.

Over the years, things got so bad between my mother and me that we communicated by putting Ann Landers articles on the refrigerator.

- Dear Ann, My teenage daughter has become hostile and verbally abusive. Please help.
- Dear Ann, My mother won't let me walk alone to school which is across the street and I'm 16! Please help.
- Dear Ann, The crossing guard drinks. Please help.

"The level of neurosis."
(Mother of one, professor, Reform)

Growing up, I never knew why my mother was so neurotic, but as soon as she started her latest harangue, I would turn up the volume on our giant black-and-white Zenith TV set, which took up half the living room, and pretend I was somewhere else. We didn't have color TV because my mother had read somewhere that color TV sets emitted radiation. Thank G-d remotes were invented; it would have been nearly impossible to get up to change the channel with those heavy lead aprons she would have undoubtedly made us wear. My favorite programs were the family shows like *The Brady Bunch* and *The Partridge Family*. I would watch them, mouth agape. The siblings liked each other. They actually spoke to each other and had family meetings. They took care of each other. Now, granted, my brother and sister were a year apart and much older than me, but I longed to have the relationship Cindy had with Marcia or Greg. I was also obsessed with Mary Tyler Moore because she was so independent and didn't have her mother living with her, and her best friend was a loud-mouth Jewish New Yorker named Rhoda. Mary created her own family made up of friends, and I always imagined that's how my life would be. I also lived for variety shows, and the seventies seemed to have an endless parade of them, like *Laugh-In, The Sonny and Cher Comedy Hour, Donny and Marie,* and later the subversive *Saturday Night Live.* And of course, I loved watching the comedians—Totie Fields, Phyllis Diller, Joan Rivers, Johnny Carson, Gilda Radner, Steve Martin, Richard Pryor—and the talk show hosts—Mike Douglas, Merv Griffin, Dinah Shore.

After my egg-timer-allotted forty-five minutes, I would rush home and plant myself in front of the TV set while my mother made dinner. I was allowed to do this most days, except for once a month on Tuesday when my mother hosted the women from her bridge club. After sneaking a supply of the M&M's laid neatly on card tables, I would retreat upstairs into my room with a Goody hairbrush I used as a microphone. Plunking a 45 of Barbra Streisand's "Don't Rain on My Parade" on my pink and blue portable GE record player, I would scream along, imagining that my real mother, Madame Streisand, would someday come and rescue me. I would be summoned out of my reverie by my "adoptive" mother, Ruth, to "come say 'hello' to the girls"—Dottie

Tankle, Rhoda Waton, and Fran Friedman. As I heard my mother's footsteps come closer, I'd lock the door and turn up the volume full blast. When she began to pound on my door, I'd swear to myself that when I grew up I would be nothing like my overanxious mother.

When we asked the women across the country, "What makes a Jewish mother different from a non-Jewish mother?", I would look deeply into each woman's eyes and think, Prove me wrong. Please tell me that you're nothing like my mother. Invariably, they were, but all for very different reasons.

"The quintessential Jewish mother is similar to the Italian or Irish Catholic mother. She is someone who loves her children and who tries to bring them up in a way that enriches them spiritually and emotionally."
(Mother of three, volunteer, Conservative)

It took me years to find out the source of my mother's neurosis and fear, but when I was a child, her behavior seemed inexplicable. And I often wondered whom other little girls who couldn't stand their mothers looked up to. So I asked them.

#2

Who is your favorite famous Jewish woman?

"Mel Brooks."

OF ALL THE YENTAS IN THE WORLD, my mother's friend had to name that one, a man no less, but no matter, everyone had a favorite. The old lefties said Bella Abzug; the Zionists always said Golda Meir. Everyone mentioned the triptych—Bette, Barbara (Walters, that is), and Barbra (Streisand, of course). Occasionally, the older women would search through their memories for a long-forgotten actress. Whenever we'd get stuck, we'd call my mother. She could rattle off a name, whether it was Sylvia Sidney, Belle Barth, Gertrude Berg as the incomparable Molly Goldberg, or her old classmate at Julia Richmond High School in New York City, Betty Joan Perske (aka Lauren Bacall). My mother was better than a stack of old *Photoplays*. She also loved the Rat Pack. When Frank Sinatra died, she called me up and said, "Another one of my cohorts—gone."

I shouted into the phone, "Yeah, Ma, that was some Rat Pack—Frank, Sammy, Dean—and Ruth."

I, however, had my own idols. Growing up in the seventies, there were two Jewish women who had challenged the mores of society and ultimately were responsible for the feminist revolution. They were Betty Friedan and Gloria Steinem. My mother quietly appreciated what they were doing, but she would always say, "Why are they drawing so much attention to themselves? Why do they have to talk about equal rights so much?"

Truth be told, my mother is fiercely pro-choice, and yet she belonged to the generation that defined itself by rigid gender roles. My father went to work. My mother took care of the home. I, of course, was a rebel. I was a ten-year-old tomboy who was rooting for Billie Jean King to wallop Bobby Riggs in their great tennis match, "Battle of the Sexes" (and so, incidentally, was my mother). The year after I was born, 1963, Betty Friedan published *The Feminine Mystique,* which outlined the exasperating lives of so many American women who tried to, but could not, find happiness through the successes of their husbands and children. The same year, Steinem published "I Was a Playboy Bunny," reporting on her three-week stint as an underpaid sexually harassed waitress. To be quite honest, back then if I had to pick between the two of them, I would have picked Steinem. Mostly because she partied at Studio 54, wore designer clothes, and made feminism seem, well, glamorous. She seemed more a movie star than a feminist icon. Betty Friedan had that angry housewife edge, with clothes to match. (And I knew there was nothing to idolize about the angry housewife; I was already living with her.)

My favorite Jewish woman famous person was, of course, Barbra Streisand. For me, Barbra was not just an actress who could sing, she was someone who had escaped a rotten childhood, had a dream, a big schnozz, was told that she was ugly, but still wouldn't take no for an answer. She managed to become one of the most powerful women in show business. I read in a biography that her stepfather would always berate her. "You're the ugly one," he would say to her over and over again, and Barbra would retreat into her own private world where she was a star. As a child and adolescent, I was riveted by *Funny Girl, Funny Lady,* and *The Way We Were,* which my mother found a cautionary tale of a nice Jewish girl marrying a *shegitz.* "The mixed marriages never work. Never," she would say rather unconvincingly as she sat, transfixed, watching the big make-out scene between Streisand and Redford on the beach.

Barbra also produced and starred in her own TV variety specials, *My Name Is Barbra* and *Color Me Barbra.* There was no doubt about it, for me, Barbra was my feminist icon. And when VCRs first came out, I begged my father to get one to enable me to indulge my Barbra obsession almost to a full-fledged madness. As soon as I was old enough, I got my mother to drive me to the Rialto Theater in Westfield to see my idol's latest. She would make me carry my birth certificate with me, because at twelve, I was almost six feet tall and the ticket takers always thought I was lying about my age. I would ask for a child's ticket, and they would look at me and look at the birth certificate and then look back at me in disbelief.

My height, or rather my enormous capacity to grow, mystified my mother. Granted, we were not a short family, but I seemed to be an anomaly even among them. During one of my yearly visits to the pediatrician, my mother said (trying to keep the panic out of her voice), "Tell her, Doctor, how people would kill to have her height." The doctor mumbled a couple of words about basketball and modeling as I squirmed in a way-too-small examination gown. After this rather bizarre pep talk (of which I did not believe a single word), my mother asked me to wait outside while she talked to the doctor alone. I stood outside the door and heard her, unable to contain her anxiety any longer, shout, "WHEN is it going to stop?"

My height, as you can imagine, did not make me popular growing up. I couldn't wear the same clothes as the girls in my class. I towered over the boys, which threatened their nascent manhood to no end. My classmates called me Sasquatch and Bigfoot and would shout at me, "How's the weather up there?" I spent a lot of time playing the piano at home. My brother had a tape recorder that he used to practice his haftorah on for his Bar Mitzvah. I took it and recorded songs from the radio. I would play and sing along for hours. One day in class, they asked if anyone would like to accompany the class on piano for graduation. The class was singing a Seals & Crofts song. I raised my hand and auditioned. Afterward, all the kids who thought I was such a loser came up to me and said, "I didn't know you could play the piano. I thought it was the teacher playing." It was my first inkling that perhaps social acceptance could come from performing. Of course, when the graduation recital ended (we graduated in size order, I was the last one to graduate), the tall jokes started again, but it planted a seed in me. Maybe I could get out of Clark, New Jersey, and be someone, just like my idol Barbra.

"Sophie Tucker. Bette Midler. Joan Rivers."
(Mother of two, writer, Reform)

When the movie *Yentl* came out, I was already in college, and yet I still spent weeks lip-synching "Papa, Can You Hear Me?" I recorded the album onto a cassette and played it over and over again in the car and in my dorm room at Rutgers University.

Before mid-semester break freshman year, I discovered

two things: stand-up comedy and Santa Claus. There was a tradition in our dorm for everyone to pick a Secret Santa. Now, usually this involves a benign task and then an exchange of gifts, but our Secret Santa was the Jewish version, so it was ultracompetitive. The first note from my Secret Santa told me to dress for church, sing "O Come All Ye Faithful," and give a speech about the Immaculate Conception. (How Mary managed to pull that one off with Joseph is still a mystery to me.) The following morning a second note appeared under my door instructing me to do five minutes of stand-up comedy. That day I cut my classes and spent the entire day writing material. That night in the lounge, I performed what would be my first stand-up set, and I killed. I was higher than a kite. After that, I began to perform on open mic nights at the college pub, and anywhere else that would have me.

When I graduated, I went over and auditioned for the master's program at Rutgers' Mason Gross School of the Arts. I was told by the department chair, Bill Esper, that I was talented, but that I was too tall and he would never be able to cast me in anything. One would think that would have stopped me, but I took it as a challenge. I mean, wasn't Barbra Streisand told that she was too ugly? Didn't she still get all those ingenue parts? She inspired me to move to New York City and take a chance on pursuing my dream. I have to say, if I hadn't had a role model like Barbra, I probably would still be in Clark, New Jersey, living out the Jewish version of *Grey Gardens* with my mother:

"Is this cat food kosher, Judith?"

"Oh, Ma, please, you know I only shop at the Parve Pet!"

Instead, New York City became my graduate school. I found a roommate through the gay roommate service. (I told my parents that I was using the gay roommate service because I wanted a male roommate who would not hit on me and would be neat. That, of course, was only half the story. More later.) I wound up with a gay opera singer who, when he wasn't touring, smoked pot and ate copious amounts of Entenmann's bakery products.

I also started taking acting classes at HB Studios with Carol Rosenfeld and Stephen Strimpell. I studied theater games with Paul Sills. After a few years I heard about this acting teacher named Alice Spivak. She had a reputation for brutal honesty. She didn't let you bullshit your way through a scene. I signed up for her Monday night class, and she's been my acting coach ever since. We interviewed her during a break from her coaching job on the *Sopranos* set. Alice showed up without an ounce of makeup. There was an openness to her that separated her from the other women. It's not that she didn't care how she looked—it was as if she was saying, "This is me. This is who I am." Now in her early sixties, she had divorced when her boys were young, and she had seen it and done it all. When we asked her who her favorite famous Jewish mother was, she smiled.

"Eleanor Roosevelt. Seriously, this is going to sound crazy, but when I was growing up, Franklin Roosevelt was president. And my mother and I thought that Roosevelt was a Jewish name. My mother came from Poland, she couldn't read; I was just a little girl. My mother and I loved Eleanor Roosevelt; I used to read my mother her column that she wrote in the newspaper. She was such a wonderful person. She cared so much about people. I remember when she died, my mother and I both cried. By that time I knew she wasn't Jewish. But growing up, I thought Roosevelt was a Jewish name. I was so proud to have a First Lady who was Jewish like me—and such a good person."

Now, I loved that response because it was so sweet imagining a little girl reading to her illiterate immigrant mother. I hid most of the books I read as a child. They were all written by Judy Blume, who was our Jewish equivalent to the *goyische Little House on the Prairie* books by Laura Ingalls Wilder. The lead character in Judy Blume's books was always this tortured adolescent who hated her mother, lived in New Jersey, and was harboring some deep, dark little secret. Well, I was not only a tortured adolescent, but I was also six feet tall and played clarinet in the marching band, so I was really popular (not!). My deep, dark secret was that I knew I was gay.

I was twenty-two when I met Wendy and we fell in love. My pothead opera singer's sometime boyfriend was a coke-addicted headhunter. (Talk about multitasking.) He got me a job at Military Media, a firm that sold advertising on behalf of military base newspapers. It was run by a husband-and-wife team; she was a failed dancer, which to her meant that nobody could make it in show business; he was a WASP who seemed to spend every waking moment studying *The Preppy Handbook* (the collars on his polo shirt defied gravity). Half the office went to lunch at twelve (the straight half), and the other half, comprised of insanely bitchy gay men (otherwise known as my fan base), went to lunch at one. They got me into their 1 P.M. lunch club. An employee named Wendy, who had six months' seniority on me, complained to the failed dancer, so they moved my lunch slot to noon. I invited Wendy to lunch to see if we could sort through this misunderstanding, so I could go back to entertaining the boys. She became my instant friend. She was Mary Tyler Moore to my Rhoda. We began to have long conversations on the phone. And when I finally got up the nerve to tell her that I was gay, she hung up on me. The next morning I found a yellow Post-it on my desk that said, "I am in love with you."

If you asked my mother in the early days who Wendy was, she would say, "She's Judith's roommate. New York is very expensive and Judith is always traveling. Wendy is a lovely girl."

Wendy's mother used to say, "I don't care that Wendy is a lesbian; I just hate Judy."

Let's just say neither of our mothers belonged to PFLAG. (Parents and Friends of Lesbians and Gays) or marched in any Gay Pride Parades holding signs that said, "I love my lesbian daughter." My mother's sign would probably say, "Why me, G-d? Why?" It took years for my mother to piece together that Wendy and I were more than just roommates. It didn't matter that we lived together in a studio apartment with two cats and one queen-sized bed, with an alarm clock on each side. Although she would occasionally ask, "Does Wendy find the floor a little uncomfortable for her back?"

After Wendy and I moved into a two-bedroom apartment, that "big scene" finally happened. For my straight readers, the "big scene" is the one that happens when you come out to your parents. (In this case it was my mom, as my father had died two years before.) After countless invitations, my mother showed up at my apartment with her 1975 El Al Tour of Israel and the Holy Land bag, and said, "I don't want to kick Wendy out of her room." I walked her to the second bedroom—you know, the one with the daybed with a week's worth of laundry on top of it and no alarm clock (the "I am not out to my parents roommate room"). I cleared the laundry off the bed, put down her bag, and said, "You're not kicking Wendy out of her bedroom." And then she did what all Jewish mothers do—she ignored the elephant in the middle of the living room and started in on the cats. "Judith, Martina won't look at me, but Billie Jean, she doesn't leave me alone. Enough of the licking, Billie, enough! That tongue—it's like sandpaper. Judith! I thought you had Martina de-clawed. G-d, will you look at what she did to my nylons? Oh, G-d. Get her off! Judith!"

A few nights later, when Wendy was out of town, my friend Joe came to dinner. Joe had just gotten married, so my mother asked him if he knew anyone for me. Joe being Joe, he said, "Sure, Mrs. Gold, she could marry my brother and keep Wendy on the side." After he left, my mother slammed the door so hard that my entire collection of Jodie Foster movies fell off the shelf, and turned to me in a rage. "And keep Wendy on the side. I knew it! This is why I'm so depressed. This is part of my problem. You."

The next day I found a freshly clipped Ann Landers column on the refrigerator. It read, "Dear Ann, my daughter has recently told me she is a lesbian. Signed, Why is she doing this to me?"

3

Do you approve of your children's choices?

"There are certain questions I will not answer, and that's one of them."

THIS WAS MY MOTHER'S ANswer when Kate asked her this question. Last year, I received a call from *Nightline* because I had submitted an essay about when I discovered that I was a lesbian, for a collection of essays entitled *When I Knew*. They wanted me with one of my parents. I told them, "Okay, my father's dead, so unless you have a remarkable hair and makeup department, your other option is my mother."

Honestly, I did not know if she would do it, because she's so negative about everything. So I called her, and she said, "I do not know why we have to discuss it. It's not my cup of tea. Then I go to the grocery store and everyone is staring at me."

"Ma, they're looking at you because you are in the motor scooter bashing into everyone in the produce section. Melons are flying all over the place. That's why they are staring at you. Not because I'm a lesbian. And maybe if you stopped wearing those huge sunglasses the doctor gave you in 1989 after your cataract surgery, it would help." (She looks like Bea Arthur as a welder.) She finally agreed to do the interview after my brother told her to. Her only condition was that we tape it at her house.

The day of the taping, I asked who else would be on the show. They were all mothers with their gay sons. They identified each other as best friends, and the mothers spoke about how thrilled they were that their sons were gay, and how they redecorated their apartments and got mani-pedis together, etc. Then there was us—Joan and Melissa without the surgery and without the red carpet. Before the interview, my mother asked me a question I never thought I'd hear. I mean, after almost twenty years of never discussing the elephant in the middle of the room, she asked, "When *did* you know, Judith?"

"WHAT?"

"When did you know?"

"I don't know," I said. "I knew when I was, like, three, but I didn't know what it was until I was like eleven or twelve?"

My mother shot back, "I knew before you."

"WHAT?!" I said.

"Oh, I knew when you were two. Every night you'd go over to the neighbors', to use their crayons." (Yes, G-d forbid she should buy me a box of crayons, lest I could potentially mess up the house.) "But you had to wear a necktie."

"WHAT?!"

"Yes, before you left the house, you'd put on one of your father's neckties."

"Wait a minute, if I was a cross-dressing two-year-old, why did you act so surprised when you found out I was gay?"

"Judith, I'm so dizzy. Will you get me a glass of water?"

I don't know why I still keep hoping she's going to say something like "I love my children unconditionally, and whatever makes them happy is okay with me." Most of the women we interviewed said, "I absolutely approve of what they want to do," and then added, "unless of course I disapprove, then I let my opinions be known."

At our first set of interviews, we met an Orthodox woman in her mid-sixties. She was immaculately dressed in a plaid St. John knit suit. Her blond wig was elegant and cut beautifully. Only after a closer look could we tell that it was not her real hair. She sat straight up with her back barely touching the chair. Unlike the other women, she wasn't nervous. She met my gaze with a steely reserve that unnerved me. It was as if she were saying, "You've met your match with me, my dear." After a sip of coffee, she began:

"You cannot know what it is like to be a mother until you are one. So it's easy to criticize a situation when you are not in it." (She took a sip of water and caught my eye.) "I didn't always approve of my daughter's choices, but now I do. You see, my daughter was spending time with someone I really didn't like. I don't know why I didn't like him. I just knew he was not the right one. Yes, he was Jewish, but he was all wrong. My husband said, 'Get rid of him.' It took a few months, but I felt I had to save her from this. If my daughter was crossing the street and I saw a car coming, I would try and save her. So why shouldn't I save her now? How did I do it? When the boy called, I would be cold and I would not give my daughter the message. I didn't welcome him into our home. Ever. I was so rude that his rabbi called to find out what I had against him. I just knew this was the wrong thing for her to do. And in the end I did it. I shattered the relationship. It's a big chance you take, maybe even losing your daughter's love. But, until this day, I know I was right. I have three lovely grandchildren and a son-in-law I adore. He's a doctor."

I wonder what I would do if Henry or Ben were dating someone I didn't like. Would I interfere? A few weeks later we found out that this woman's daughter never did forgive her mother for what she did.

After that interview, I felt discouraged because many of

these women were confirming all my worst fears about Jewish mothers. Also, these interviews were only supposed to be twenty to thirty minutes, but they were going on for hours. I don't know what we were thinking, because there's absolutely no way any Jewish mother can answer twenty-five questions in a half hour.

"I absolutely approve of what they want to do."
(Mother of two, art historian, nonpracticing)

While on the whole more of the women surprised us than disappointed us, what we didn't expect was the impact these interviews had on their husbands. We had not imagined in the slightest that the men would be interested in the emotional lives of their wives.

After one particularly grueling set of interviews, we were headed out the door and we saw a husband in his sixties sitting on the stairs. As we were walking out the door, he motioned toward us and then whispered, "I've known these women for over thirty years. And tonight after hearing what they had to say, I realized that I don't really know them at all."

It hit me at that moment. Not only were these women being asked about their lives for the first time, but their husbands were also hearing what they had to say for the first time. And it wasn't only the husbands. One night Kate nudged me and pointed up. Three boys ranging in age from ten to fifteen were sitting with their legs between the banisters, listening. Their father had come to shoo them back into their rooms, but instead had joined his sons. For the first time in a long time, these men and boys were seeing their wives and mothers as people with hopes and dreams, that they had a life outside of being a wife and mother. Is that why they were so invested in their children's lives? It seemed that women in their sixties and above were more inclined to interfere with their adult children than mothers in their forties. In the latter group, the women were more inclined to take a backseat and keep their mouths shut simply because their lives had been so overrun by their own mothers.

> *"If there are some things that I see that are not to my liking sometimes, but if it is between a husband and wife, I would not interfere. I just keep quiet."*
> (Mother of five, homemaker, Orthodox)

A mother's interference isn't always negative. One mother we spoke to had interfered with her son's life in an amazing way. The wife of an Orthodox rabbi, she saw her son struggling and realized that she could sit back and do nothing or make a choice and help him.

"My second child has a learning disability. Years ago no one knew anything about learning disabilities, and it was very hard for us to accept, because my other children were very bright and overachievers. My husband would get up at five in the morning to go over a test with him. I said this is pointless. If he knows a little bit more about the Bible or less, it's not important. We really have to teach him life skills. But there were no Orthodox yeshivas for a child that was not perfect. So I went back to school and got a master's degree in special education. My husband really encouraged me. I had four little kids, but he insisted that I go back to school and he did all the babysitting. I became a teacher, and recently I retired as principal of a school for children with learning disabilities. My son married someone who is also slow. They have no children, but they enjoy each other's company. So there is more than one happy ending to this story."

Having a child who was different changed this woman's life. But about some women, especially the ones who seemed unfulfilled, I wondered what they would have done if they had not had children.

4

Would your life have taken a different turn if you hadn't had children?

"I would have gone to Nashville and become a country-and-western singer."
(Mother of two, disgruntled housewife, Reform)

OKAY, THAT'S A JEWISH COUNTRY-and-western singer. That's like misery cubed. Can you imagine that song? "You took a fine time to leave me, Schlemiel!"

We asked my mother the same question. She actually said, "I would do what you do. I'd be a stand-up comic."

WHAT?!? Can you imagine that routine? Spotlight, please. Here comes my mother walking on stage moaning about her knees, wearing a lovely shul dress, knocking down the mic. As she bends down, holding her lower back, whispering "son of a bitch" under her breath, she picks up the mic, after she figures out how to disengage it from the stand, and taps it several times shouting, "IS IT ON?" And then after a long sigh, she begins her "set."

RUTH—So, how's everyone doing tonight? My name is Ruth, or Rivkah if you're a member of the tribe. (At this point my mother glares at the audience for a response.) So, you know what I was thinking the other day? It's a good thing that the Jews aren't into the drugs. Because if you really think about it, Jewish mothers would make the best drug pushers.

"You don't like the crack? Fine, don't smoke it!" (Shaking her fist at the imaginary child, meaning me.)

"My back is killing me. (Grabbing her back as if writhing in pain.) I've been slaving over the stove all day cooking up this crystal meth and you won't even touch it."

(Then as if her final try.) "I cut some heroin nice and thin with the baby powder the way you like it, Schnookey. Wipe your nose." Thank you. That's it for me. I'll be here all week. Try the veal. Use the side exit and don't forget to tip your waitress. Seven, six, two percent is fine. It's not like they made the drinks. I'm sure most of them can't even add. If they could add they wouldn't be working in this hellhole. So long.

"Sure, I'd be a published author by now."
(Mother of two, wife of a rabbi, Conservative)

I always knew I wanted to be a performer. When I was a kid, I would imitate everyone from the cashier at Pathmark to the rabbi's wife to Lauren Bacall doing those gravelly throated Brim coffee commercials—"Fill it to the rim with Brim." After I met Wendy, I used to brag, "You know, I used to do stand-up at Rutgers." After the twentieth time I said this, Wendy looked at me and said in that sweet, insistent voice of hers, "Either stop talking about it already or just go back and do it." Well, that stopped me in my tracks. I had to put up or shut up.

Wendy had this gift for being able to separate her work life and her private life—I think one would call that "having boundaries." Well, as you can imagine, I had (I mean have) none. She was my perfect partner because she was able to read people on a different level than I was able to do. When I first started going to the clubs, I made Wendy come with me. She would sit at the bar and take notes, all the while taking in the atmosphere. "You know, it seems like the bartender has some influence—make friends with him . . ." She was my eyes and ears. All I cared about was getting on stage and getting laughs, and she was the business part of show business. After I started to feel comfortable enough to hang at the clubs by myself, I would leave work, spend some time with Wendy, and then I was off to the clubs every night.

There wasn't a better or more magical time to be a comic than in the mid-eighties and early nineties. Comedy always flourishes during Republican administrations, and during Reagan, it exploded. There was an endless array of places to perform. Catch a Rising Star on First between Seventy-seventh and Seventy-eighth, Comic Strip on Second between Eighty-first and Eighty-second, Caroline's, Comedy U Grand in Soho, and of course, the Improv at Forty-fourth and Ninth. On any given night, Jerry Seinfeld, Joy Behar, Larry David, Carol Leifer, Margaret Smith, Steven Wright, Richard Belzer, Susie Essman, and Paula Poundstone would all be performing around the city. I would go to all of the clubs on open mic night, while Wendy stood in the back with Anna, Ray Romano's wife. At that time Ray's daytime job was delivering futons across the city. I remember one night Anna saying to me, "Do you really think this is worth it? Do you really think he's going to be able to make a living doing this?" Now it seems every time I turn on the television, *Everybody Loves Raymond* is on.

> "I would have been a vice president of a corporation. One of the big ones."
> (Mother of three, bookkeeper, Orthodox)

Chasing a dream in New York City is both intoxicating and exhausting. I would work the clubs until 3 A.M., get up at seven, and go to my job as a typesetter. (I had left Military Media so that I could have more flexibility and get paid enough money to afford health insurance. Going to doctors is kind of like a hobby for me; after all, I am my mother's daughter. My goal is to make my way through the entire issue of *New York* magazine's Best Doctors issue. I am up to O for orthopedic surgeons.)

I'd come home at six, chow down a pint of cold sesame noodles, which at that time were only $2.95 for a quart, take a nap, and start bouncing from club to club. Now, I wish I could say I started at Catch a Rising Star, but every young comic has to pay her dues, and I was no exception. So at the beginning of the evening I might start at Campus Lounge on Wall Street, then go do a set at this Indian restaurant on Forty-second Street that had a bug zapper over my head on the stage. (At least I was assured of some reaction to my jokes.) From there, I would head up to the Improv, where Chris Albrecht, now chairman and CEO of HBO, ran the door, then down to Comedy U Grand. The better-known clubs would let the young comics on later in the evening after all the regulars had done their sets. I would pray that the four drunks in the audience would stay so that I could get some stage time. You could take whatever risks you wanted on stage at that time because nobody was watching.

After about a year (which is *not* a lot of time in comedy land) of nonstop hustling, I finally got "passed" at Catch a Rising Star, which meant that I could sign up for spots on the chart. Then on Tuesday, they would call and give you your actual spot times. All the up-and-coming comics, and some of the better known ones, would sit by the phone, waiting obsessively for the call on Tuesday afternoon. Then we would all call each other and ask, "Have they finished the schedule? Did you get a spot? I got a nine-fifteen on Thursday," or "Wait!!! He's on the schedule?! He just passed last week!"

When you got that call, you knew you had your foot on the ladder. It might be the bottom rung, but it was a step higher than brushing dead flies out of your hair from the bug zapper at the Indian restaurant. I got to be a "backup" at Catch a Rising Star. I would get paid to sit at the bar during the weekend shows just in case a comic missed or was late for his or her spot—I would be there to go on in his or her place. The other backup was this really nice young comic named—Chris Rock. We got paid $50 per weekend show—which was a lot. Back then we only got paid cab fare during the week ($10–15 per set)—that has just increased to $20–25.

The problem with that life was I didn't spend any consistent time at home. I would be hanging out with Wendy watching TV, and then at 10 P.M., I'd have to get up off of the sofa and put on my makeup to go to a set. Wendy understood my unyielding ambition, even though it offered her nothing in the way of reliability. We would plan a weekend away, or a night out, and inevitably I would get a call offering me work. I had to take everything I could get. She spent most weekends without me, waiting in the back of the club, or meeting me for a half hour in between spots. She went to parties alone, and although she was disappointed, more often than not, she was very supportive. She had lots of her own ambition and an amazing work ethic. She started as an editor for a medical journal and ended up as a marketing executive and eventually a division president of a huge advertising agency. We would argue some about my schedule, but my work always won out.

"I'd have gone to law school."
(Mother of three, paralegal, Conservative)

In order to make decent money in the city, I'd have to do anywhere from three to seven shows per night, but the real money came from going on the road. You needed fifteen minutes of solid material to be an opening act, thirty minutes to be the middle, and forty-five to headline. And you only became a headliner when no one could follow you, you got a TV show, you did *The Tonight Show,* or your name could sell tickets.

I'll never forget one of the first times I "middled" at a decent club. It was the last time my father got to see me perform. I was working at the Catch a Rising Star in Princeton, New Jersey. He drove out there with my mother. A few weeks later he was dead of a massive coronary after swimming laps. I was twenty-seven years old, my career was just beginning, and I had missed my father's last Father's Day so that I could work. I was so sad, and didn't know how I was going to be able to go out on stage and be funny again. But I knew that my father would have wanted me to follow my dream. At the end of sitting shiva (think Irish wake with turkey, corned beef, pastrami, coleslaw, potato salad, rye bread, Russian dressing, noodle kugel, black-and-white cookies, kosher wine instead of Rolling Rock), the family takes a walk around the block together to show they are ready to reenter society not as mourners. I took that walk with my mother and my sister, and knew it was time to continue with my life even though I was still grieving inside.

I dealt with my grief by going on the road. My father's death totally changed my act. I was way more fearless on stage. No one was going to have any power over me because nothing could affect me as much as my father's death. I wasn't scared to discuss sensitive issues, and I was way more edgy.

I was single-minded in my determination to say kaddish

every Saturday for my father. So, no matter where I was, I would look up a synagogue. It was a blessing in disguise. (No pun intended.) I actually looked forward to that time on Saturday morning, because even though I was all alone in a strange city, I recognized those prayers and melodies and it made me feel safe. I would look around at the people, and for some reason their faces looked familiar, and I felt that I could go to any one of their homes and know exactly what was in their refrigerators. I would always call my mother after services, still expecting my father to answer the phone. I missed him terribly.

As my career flourished, my relationship with Wendy began to suffer. We started to fight. She was very focused on her career as well, but she had "regular" hours and I worked from the minute I woke up until I went to sleep. I wanted to be on stage more than I wanted to be anywhere else, and sadly that included home. I loved Wendy so much. She was my confidante, my best friend, and my anchor. She grounded me. Whenever I was rejected, mistreated, or put down, she was always there to put things into perspective. We had this life that, when I think back, was akin to Bill and Hill. I mean we were the ultimate partners—there for each other on every level, through thick and thin. We were each other's family because, G-d knows, our families would never ever be able to understand us.

Despite my hectic schedule, Wendy was determined to have a baby, but I just wasn't ready. Every night I would call her from the road, and every night it would be the same thing: "Judy, I want to have a baby." I would respond, "Well, let me just get to where I want to be in my career and then we can talk about it."

One year on my birthday, I was headlining for the first time in Winnipeg, Canada. It was the middle of winter (don't be jealous) and Wendy called, and this time she said, "You know what? I'm having this kid with or without you." And then she hung up. I called her back and I lost it. (See, calling home for a comedian is kind of like warming up.)

"Hi. How many times do I have to go over this? But I'm not ready to have a child! I thought we had this resolved. Don't say fuck you to me. Why? Well, fuck you then. No, *you* go fuck yourself."

I slammed down the phone and then I walked on stage to do my set. I usually don't let anything, let alone my home life, affect my act in a negative way. I can turn almost anything around and make it funny, but not that night. I was so angry and depressed that I turned on my audience. I noticed a very nice-looking Canadian couple holding hands and looking at me with those "It's Saturday night, please make us laugh; the babysitter is costing us a fortune" eyes. And of course I started chatting them up. "It's great to be here in Winterpeg. Canada. In the middle of winter. It's cold, isn't it?" They nodded politely and smiled that "Oh, she's talking to us; how exciting" smile. I glared at their happy faces and continued, "I went outside the other day for five minutes, and I've got three fingers left. Guess I have to cancel my piano recital and my hand modeling job next week. The city is quite nice, though. Yesterday I was driving around with my sherpa and tried to give someone the finger. But I couldn't!"

My charming and polite couple chuckled a bit. The cold, yes, it was cold. She's right. And I could have stopped there, but instead I took my mic and I began to scream, "Why the fuck do you people live here? You have to plug your car in to start it. Your beer sucks. You suck. And you can all go fuck yourselves."

My happy Canadian couple stopped smiling. I had gone too far with the beer dig. Before they pummeled me with their hockey sticks, I shouted quickly, "Thank you very much. I'll be here all week. Try the veal. Tip your waitress."

I got off stage and went immediately into the greenroom. The opening act sat down next to me and said, "Look, I heard you talking on the phone to Wendy before." He pulled out a photo of his two daughters and said, "You know, Judy, there's always an excuse not to have children . . . But they are what make nights like this bearable."

I didn't want to lose Wendy, and I had always imagined

having a family of my own. I certainly couldn't imagine my life without Wendy. So I called her back after the second show (which went a little better) and I said, "Hi, just want to let you know, you're having this kid *with* me."

I know now that if I hadn't had kids, that would've been my biggest regret.

#5

What's your biggest regret?

"The unspoken pressure I put on my girls to do it all." (Mother of two, psychologist, Reform)

THIS QUESTION USUALLY ELICITED A ONE-SENTENCE RE-sponse like the answer above. Most of the women would not even admit they had regrets. It was almost as if they were afraid to voice them, lest someone think badly of them or that they weren't grateful for what they had. Some kept repeating, "I'm happy with my life. I have no regrets." But when we would probe deeper, there was always a wish unfulfilled or a dream undiscovered.

Jewish mothers, by their very definition, make an art of self-sacrifice. At first, I was hesitant to even ask them this question because it seemed so personal. I mean, that's a big thing to admit to a stranger, but the one woman who really opened up to me changed my whole outlook on this project. And this woman was not born Jewish, but had in fact con-verted as a condition of her marriage. Unlike her friends, she wasn't dripping with diamonds or shod in Prada, but was clad in a modest pale violet twinset, a single strand of pearls, and a black above-the-knee skirt. But it was not just the simplicity of her style that made her stand apart from her friends.

"My biggest regret? People have asked me, do I regret converting? Well, there are a lot of parallels between being Jewish and being Chinese. In Chinese culture sons are revered and girls are second-class citizens. And the number one rule they share is—Don't embarrass me in public. I am from both cultures. Honest. I am a modern Orthodox Chinese Jewish woman. I am the second daughter of Chinese immigrants. I am a rebel. I met my husband in a bookstore in San Francisco, and after a couple of dates he said, 'I would like to marry someone Jewish.' So I found an Orthodox rabbi in Berkeley and studied with him for two years and then we got married. Afterwards, I would run into my mother's friends, who would say, 'Theresa, I have boy for you.' She had told no one I had gotten married. I remained an embarrassment to my mother until her death. Even though I was the only one of her six children to graduate from college. After my marriage, I worked as a social worker in San Francisco. I did a lot of home care visits to the elderly. I knocked on one door. A woman opened it and she said to me, 'Mrs. Weinstein?' and I said

to her, 'Mrs. Wong?' You see, she was white—and I'm Chinese. It's not often you find someone living your parallel life. I loved San Francisco; I hated leaving it. My husband wanted us to come to New Jersey. He wanted the kids to go to Jewish school here, and he said that we wouldn't stand out so much. But the truth is I never felt like a minority until I came here. One man shouted at me, 'Hey, Chink!' I said to him, 'Are you talking to me?' He said, 'Yeah, don't you know who you are?' But that's not who I am. I don't ever regret converting to Judaism, but I regret moving here. I hate New Jersey. I don't belong here."

Finally someone I could relate to! I didn't belong in New Jersey either. I hated growing up there because I felt like such an outsider. And if our mothers weren't completely ashamed by our "lifestyles," they were at least embarrassed by who and what we had become. Besides being a Chinese convert, she was also a Democrat in a largely Republican community. In the midst of her interview something unexpected happened; another woman walked in and sat down. I looked at my watch; the next interview wasn't scheduled for another half hour. She planted herself in a chair by the door and waved at us as if to say, "Don't mind me." Kate leaned over and whispered "I'll ask her to leave" to the woman we were interviewing. But she shook her head and continued recounting, in a brutally honest way, how unhappy she was. At one point she confessed, "Sometimes I feel like I am going to throw myself in front of a bus." Later, Kate saw the two women in the corner talking. The first woman—who had seemed so unhappy an hour ago—was smiling and talking to the second woman, who we found out was a psychologist.

On the drive home, as we were rehashing the interviews, I said to Kate, "You know, I think this project is also about building a community among women. Maybe we should let them listen to each other. I mean, the men are listening in."

"The men need to listen," Kate pointed out.

We talked it through some more, and from that moment on we gave the women a choice: "Do you mind if other women listen? Or would you like for us to talk to you alone?" This question was not really a choice when we interviewed my mother and her friends. Because my mother is not very mobile, asking her to leave the house wasn't really an option. She stayed in the back room paging through the *New York Times* with her sullen nurse's aide. Before each woman arrived, my mother would shout from her wheelchair and warn us, "Now, remember, do not mention the youngest son, or the one that had that terrible divorce, or the biracial granddaughter. And absolutely under any circumstances do not mention her brother and the embezzlement."

Inevitably, after a couple of rugelach and a mug of coffee, the women would begin to spill everything about their lives, whether it be broken marriages, disappointing children, or secret longings.

My mother, however, did not talk about her personal life at all during our interview. Would she have been more candid if only Kate had interviewed her and I hadn't been there? I'm not sure. It wasn't just the gay thing (which she would not even discuss). There was something about her that was extremely cautious. "It's like she's got this door, Jude. Every time I think I have the right key, she deadbolts the lock," Kate whispered as we got ready to leave. "And, Jude, what's with the six quarts of frozen milk in the freezer?"

"It's in case of a snowstorm," I said, giving her a quick course in Jew logic. "And what were you doing in my mother's freezer?"

"Jude, it's July. I wanted some ice for my Tab. And FYI, those cans looked like they were from the seventies."

"I didn't put more self-confidence in my children. If a teacher complained, I took the teacher's side."
(Mother of four, homemaker, Orthodox)

Did my mother ever take my side? I don't know. I know she loved me as well as she could. After she found out I was gay, I was careful what I told her about my life. The army borrowed their "don't ask, don't tell" policy from my relationship with my mother. I do have to say that she was incredibly nice to Wendy, and made sure to include her on the holidays and family occasions, but she was not happy about what she deemed my "lifestyle." So when Wendy and I were trying to get pregnant, I certainly did not rush to tell her. I decided not to tell her until we actually were, and the truth was, after a year of trying, we weren't any closer to parenthood.

At that time, I was playing Vegas, when my then manager called and said that she was leaving the management business. I panicked, because a comedian depends on a manager for bookings and also for finding the right kinds of projects. And being a six-foot-three Jewish female comedian, I needed all the help I could get.

I didn't tell my mother (who was in Vegas keeping me company and giving me material), because I knew that she would immediately voice my biggest fears. "Well, now what?!? What are you gonna do? Can you get another manager? How are you going to get work?" So I kept the bad news to myself—an example of my "If she asks, don't tell and then she won't yell" policy. I called my good friend and fellow comedian Bob Smith, and he suggested that I meet with his managers, which I did. The same day I met with them, I auditioned for a sitcom called *All American Girl* starring stand-up comedian Margaret Cho. It was a rather inspired comedy about a young, second-generation Korean American, torn between two very different cultures.

At the audition, I was asked if I was going to be in town for the next few weeks. Now, rule number one for the baby comics out there—always say yes. (Doesn't matter if you're leaving for the Peace Corps or prison, you always say yes at an audition.) The following day I left to perform for a week on a male-only gay cruise. It was my first cruise, and I was so excited—what better way to spend your first cruise than with a bunch of hot, fun, gay men. Two days later I got a message under my cabin door to call my new managers immediately. I called, and they began shouting, "You've got to fly home. They want to send you to network." Network is the final part in the audition process. It's when the big executives decide who is going to get the part. I was reading for Margaret Cho's best friend. Why they thought it would be funny if the diminutive Asian girl had a six-foot-three Jewish girl as her sidekick is beyond me. In order to play the Ethel to her Lucy, I had to get off the ship and fast. The closest port was in Colombia. Granted, my experience of the Third World was limited, but being escorted at gun-point to a bug-infested hotel and checking in with a SWAT team terrified me.

The next day at the airport I boarded the plane to LA, and I got the part. I shot the pilot and waited to hear if the show got picked up. Wendy and I were taking a nap when my agent called to say congratulations. I couldn't believe it! I did it! We flew out to LA to look for a place, and I started work on *All American Girl* in July. I loved working on a sit-com. Wendy would visit me on the weekends, and for a time she was allowed to telecommute at her job. I was making oodles of money, and it seemed like we had it all. While shooting the show, I still continued to do stand-up, which was as essential to me as breathing. It fed my psyche, and I didn't want to get lazy. Before I got cast on *All American Girl*, HBO was putting together a special called *Women of the Night* featuring a few select female comics. I was desperate to be chosen. I wasn't. But I did set up an audition for a friend of mine named Carol Henry. She was chosen to do the show. Carol was one of those people who could make me laugh uncontrollably. We would sit on the phone for hours after we got home from the clubs just cracking each other up. Naturally, I wished I had been chosen, but I was truly excited for her. Carol was HIV+, and I knew she was running out of time.

While I was doing *All American Girl*, HBO offered me my own half-hour special, which was to be filmed at the great old Fillmore Auditorium in San Francisco. I was on the same bill as Jonathan Katz and Janeane Garofalo. My mother flew in from New York to be in the audience. At the end of my set, they filmed her saying, "I hope you enjoyed the show. So long!" Now I had my own HBO special and a sitcom. I had accomplished all of that in just under ten years.

Finally I felt that I was ready to start a family, but every month it was the same thing. Wendy would take the pregnancy test and it would be negative. I kept thinking to myself, I'm ready to be a mom, so why isn't this happening? One afternoon, Wendy took the test and it was negative, so she did what she always did. She threw it in the garbage, and we went out to drown our misery with giant frozen margaritas at our favorite Mexican place in LA. The next morning, we were both cursing Jose Cuervo and his other friend, Señor Corona. When Wendy went into the bathroom, she noticed a line on the test that wasn't there before. It was red. She hadn't waited long enough before she threw it out. Wendy ran into the bedroom and screamed, "It's positive!!!!!!! I'm pregnant!!!!"

I was in shock. I had the world at my feet—or so it seemed. My mother always said after each of my successes, "Very nice." I knew when I told her that her daughter's roommate of twelve years was pregnant, it was going to elicit a less-than "very nice" retort. This was eleven years ago, before Ellen, before Rosie or Melissa Etheridge had kids. So there wasn't any *People* magazine glossy cover story I could use to help my mother understand that her lesbian daughter's partner was having a baby. I knew it wasn't going to be an easy sell, but I decided to tell my mother on *Shabbos*, because I make really great decisions.

It went something like this:

RUTH—All right, Judith, yes, you and Wendy have something very important to tell me which I would've liked to have heard AN HOUR AGO when you were supposed to be here. But, thank God, you're here before sundown. Oh, I made your favorite, the stuffed cabbage, just the way you like it. What do you mean you're not eating? What do you mean you're not hungry? Fine, don't eat it. I have some rye bread in the freezer from 1976 I can defrost. Oh, it tastes exactly the same. All right, I'm listening. Oh, by the way, I saw *Oprah* yesterday. They had on kids who were tall like you and still successful. Oprah's doing an entire week on negaholics. Neg-a-hol-ics—people who are addicted to being negative. I ordered the book. I'm not negative anymore. I've accepted this . . . situation.

So what is it that you have to tell me? I don't know, who's about to be a grandmother again? Me? Now, how is that possible? Wendy is pregnant?!! You two only think about yourselves. I don't want to interfere, but you want my advice? I'll give you my advice. *Leave me out of it.*

6

What's the best piece
of advice your mother ever
gave you?

"Never put anything in
writing." (Mother of three,
homemaker, Conservative—
aka, my mom)

MY MOTHER ALWAYS TOLD ME—
whether it be a Girl Scout cookie
form or the contract for this book—
don't put your Jane Hancock to anything. It is a piece of
advice I've thankfully ignored. Jewish mothers love to give
their children advice, but rarely admit that they do. You
know what the best advice my mother ever gave me was?
When I was thirteen, I was six feet tall and I was constantly
being teased, and my mother said to me, "Judith, don't
worry about it. They're just jealous of you. Ignore them. You
think those pipsqueaks don't wish they had your height?
Now go upstairs and take off your father's clothes." Somehow, with that one comment, my mother made me feel like
I could face one more day in Miss Ratner's homeroom.

As a mother myself, I often worry that I give too much advice to my elder son, Henry. When I was on the road a couple of years ago, Wendy told me that Henry did not want to get on the school bus. He kept having stomachaches. Finally, Henry told Wendy that he was being bullied on the bus by a fifth grader. I felt so powerless when I hung up the phone. I couldn't hug him, I couldn't protect him, I couldn't kill the kid who was doing this to him. All I could do was give him advice on how to handle it. Then I started thinking, How can I be a good mother when I'm always on the road? The more helpless I felt, the more advice I started giving Henry. Finally, after the seventeenth idea I had on how to deal with the bully, Henry said, "Mommy, it's my business and I don't want to talk about it. I'll handle it."

And he did. That didn't prevent me from calling his teacher, the bully's parents, the principal, and the bus driver, however. As time goes by, I have found out firsthand how hard it is for a Jewish mother not to interfere and give advice.

"Follow your heart."
(Mother of three, artist, Reform)

One woman we interviewed was recently divorced, and all she wanted to talk about was Jewish women and sex. She was dating a non-Jew, and her two adult daughters were incredibly upset about it. She admitted that to please her daughters she would most likely have to break up with the man she was passionately in love with. She was a woman torn between her own personal happiness and her daughters' approval. I remember her distinctly. She was in her early fifties, and her trim body was accentuated by tight-fitting black leggings. She obsessively wrapped and unwrapped a pale blue Pashmina scarf around her neck as she languorously crossed her legs in the chair. A sensuous woman, she had gone back to school and had dreams of becoming a writer. And although she was incredibly upset about her possible breakup, there was a joie de vivre about her that was infectious. After she answered the question "What's the best piece of advice your mother ever gave you?" we knew why she was the way she was.

"What's the best piece of advice that my mother ever gave me? Let me see. Ahm, yes. Be optimistic. My mother always told me that I could do anything I wanted, that I was the smartest and there was no one better, no one brighter, no one more capable. This is something that she repeated over and over again so it propelled me forward in life. I often marvel at her optimism. She used to say she was 'only in the camps for a year,' but surviving even one day was a miracle. At dawn they would line up the women naked and see who was fit for labor and who was not. My mother was

picked out of the line three times for the gas chambers by Josef Mengele. And three times she ran back to the line without them seeing her. You see if she didn't run back, she would never have been seen again, and if she was caught running, she would be shot on the spot . . . I get my optimism from my mother."

Damn! I wish my mother had told me that I could do anything. But perhaps because I didn't get her approval for the life I was living, it freed me to do a lot of things girls from my background don't necessarily do. Like bringing a baby into this world without a father.

"Believe in yourself."
(Mother of one, teacher, culturally identified)

My mother called me up a week after I told her that Wendy was pregnant. I could hear her sucking her gums through the phone line—the Jewish mother's way of displaying extreme disapproval. In a very calm but angry voice, she said, "I just have one question, Judith, WHO'S THE FATHER?"

I explained to her that we had used an anonymous sperm donor from a sperm bank. (Jewish, of course.) There was a stunned silence, I could hear more gum sucking, and finally she said, "So, what else is new?"

And then I told her that after trolling the Internet for the right donor, we ordered the sperm over the phone. And I am sure in her mind the call went something like this:

JUDY—Hi, are you delivering? Great. I'll have number 6173, the Ashkenazi doctor. Yes, does he come fresh or frozen? Great. Can I get him at least six-two? Are you doing substitutions? Fantastic. Can I substitute the acne and glasses for some musical skills and high SAT scores? Oh, and can you hold the heart disease, cancer, and depression? I have enough of that in my own family, thank you very much. Wait, hold on, let me get my Amex.

"Chew with your mouth closed."
(Mother of six, homemaker, Modern Orthodox)

Wendy used to say that all you need to get pregnant is a credit card and a doctor's appointment. Picking out the sperm is the easy part, because the truth is by the time you're ready to have a baby, your ovaries aren't. They need to be poked and prodded and threatened with fertility drugs with such friendly names as Clomid and Gonal-F. It took us nineteen tries, two and a half years, and $35,000 to get pregnant with Henry. Two and a half years. The odd thing is, if you look at women in the Bible, they all had fertility issues. Sarah gave birth at ninety. I mean how crazy is that? You know, when I'm ninety, I want to be either dead or walking around Century Village with a shopping cart enforcing the pool rules. I don't want to be breast-feeding and doing Mommy and Me classes.

7

Who is your favorite woman in the Bible?

"Mrs. Noah."

AN ELDERLY REFORM MOTHER OF THREE SAID THIS WITH A glint in her eye. "Well, think about it. Can you imagine how bad that ark must have smelled? What that woman put up with, I can't even imagine. If the Jews had saints she'd be one of them."

The answers to this question were as different as the women we spoke to. We interviewed a two-mom family in the Park Slope area of Brooklyn. Only one is Jewish, but they are raising both of their children Jewish. The mom who is Jewish is a tall, striking woman with deep blue-gray eyes. Her son is a tintype of herself. She has a dry sense of humor honed from more than twenty years of teaching in the public school system. She identifies herself as reform, but also not a particularly religious Jew. About her son's Hebrew school she comments, "I wish they would just teach him about the holidays and leave the G-d part out of it." So we were surprised when she readily answered the question about who her favorite woman in the Bible was.

"Miriam. In the Bible, God chose her along with Moses to lead the Israelites out of Egypt. She was considered a prophetess. I liked her strong and forceful nature and she was resourceful. I found her almost a feminist hero, if a feminist hero can be found in the Bible. When I first got pregnant with Theo, I told my mother and she refused to let me visit her when I started to show. She lives in this middle-class housing project in Brooklyn. She didn't want her neighbors to see me pregnant. I think, in her eyes, what I was doing was disgraceful and shameful. Then we had Theo and she went gaga. They have an incredibly strong relationship. Every Sunday, he takes the phone, puts it on speaker, and plays what he learned that week from his piano teacher. Right after he was born, I brought him over to my mother's apartment. I got on the elevator with a neighbor who had known me since I·was a little girl. She looked at Theo and then looked at me and said, 'I didn't know you got married.' And when I told her I didn't, she began to shout at me, 'If you were my daughter, I would have thrown you out.' And this went on for twenty-one floors. When I finally got to my mother's apartment, I handed Theo to my mother, and I told her about the neighbor and what she said. And my mother said, 'She's ignorant. She's sick in the head.' I took Theo back from her and I nearly shouted, 'What about you? What about you not wanting me to visit when I was pregnant?' And my mother's eyes

*filled with tears. She didn't say anything, but I knew at last
that I had made my point. I like Miriam because she led
her people through the desert, and sometimes, in a small
way when I look at my children, I feel as though I am doing
the same thing, except my desert is ignorance and intoler-
ance."*

The first people we told that Wendy was pregnant (other
than my mother) were our neighbors the Cohens, Sy and
Marjorie, who live down the hall. When we first moved in,
Marjorie passed by my door, noticed the mezuzah, and
said to me, "Are you serious about this?" I said yes. Then
she nodded and walked on. A week later, she showed up
at the door. "I saw you through the window lighting the
Shabbos candles. Do you want to come for *Shabbos* dinner
next week?" Wendy and I were nervous about going, but
we went and ended up having a wonderful dinner with
them. Marjorie is such an Upper West Side intellectual.
She dresses mostly in fitted designer jeans and black
turtlenecks. She is a voracious reader and thinker. Her two
daughters attended Ramaz, a Jewish day school on the
Upper East Side. Her husband, Sy, however, is, well, less
glamorous. Much less. Let's just say there's no glamour
there at all. He's a retired public school teacher and has a
good ten years on Marjorie. He's as Orthodox as they

come. He's as sloppy as she's meticulous. The two of them are an unlikely couple, but somehow it works. At first we were scared that they would find out we were more than roommates and would not want to be our friends. I mean, they live on the Upper West Side (where the descendants of red diaper babies routinely debate whether or not there should be a price on Ann Coulter's head), but you never know.

> *"Sarah, because she had enough gumption to tell her husband to send away his other son from his other wife."*
> *(Mother of one, actress, Reform)*

I don't know when Marjorie and Sy figured out our "situation," as my mother termed it, but when they did, they didn't mention it. They just accepted it. When we told Sy that we wanted him to be the G-dfather and Wendy was giving birth to a boy, he was thrilled. We knew he would treat him like the son he had never had.

> *"Leah, because she was the woman nobody really wanted. Jacob wanted her sister Rachel, but he got Leah. Then he treated her like dirt. Still, she became one of the founding*

> mothers in the Bible. For a woman who was
> not wanted or loved, that is an
> incredible accomplishment."
> (Mother of three, accountant, Conservative)

Henry was born a month early, on September 24, 1996. We weren't prepared. We hadn't even gotten his room ready. The doctor had told Wendy to stop working, but she begged him to let her go to the office for one more week. What did we know? The next day was Yom Kippur. I went to my mother's shul while Wendy stayed home to rest. That night we met at Marjorie and Sy's for their annual breaking of the fast. The next day, I was supposed to get on a plane to Vegas, so I was sleeping a bit later than usual. Wendy got up to get ready for work. She was loud, as usual. I put a pillow over my head and tried to drown her out. It was just starting to work when I heard her voice: "Judy, I think my water just broke. I keep dripping." I got up and looked, and said to her in my expert tone of voice, "Look, I just saw *Rescue 911* last night and this woman's water broke and it was nothing like that. It doesn't drip—it pours out." I stumbled back to bed and put the pillow back over my head. I'd been having this dream where I was hanging out with JFK Jr., and I really, really wanted to go back to it. I could vaguely hear Wendy's voice on the phone to the doctor through the pillow, but when she shouted, "Get in here immediately," I woke up.

The rest is all in this kind of fast slow motion. You know that episode of *I Love Lucy* when it's time for the baby and Ricky is running around like his head is cut off and Lucy is calmly walking out the door? Well, I was like Ricky. I was running around waving a massage wand and *People* magazine, and Wendy was calmly walking out the door. Marjorie came by and loaded us down with food from the night before. I remember she gave us this delicious *babka*. When we got to the hospital and signed in, everyone kept asking who I was in relation to Wendy, and I kept saying, "I'm her partner." They looked at me like I had three eyes. I always hated saying "partner" because it made me sound like we owned a franchise of Mail Boxes Etc. together. I was just about to be shut out of the room because I was not the husband or the abusive boyfriend or a blood relative, when a nurse walked up to me and said, "Aren't you Judy Gold?"

"Yes, I am," I replied.

"I saw you perform up in Provincetown this summer with my girlfriend. You're hilarious. Here's a wristband. Don't worry, I'll take care of you guys. Some of these nurses don't get the two-mommy thing."

I breathed a sigh of relief. She found us a beautiful, private room, and Wendy was shot up with Pitocin to induce contractions. There was only one problem. Henry wasn't supposed to be born for another month. But once that water breaks, there's no going back. We were there so long without any dilation that the nurses began to take bets on when the C-section was going to happen. Our doctor was overly attentive, so much so the nurses commented, "He really likes you two. He never comes in this much."

"Umh, hello? It's not us. It's the *babka*!"

Dr. Babka (which we renamed the doctor) and his partner, Dr. Yale, scheduled a C-section after Dr. Yale noticed the baby's heart rate plummeting whenever Wendy was having a contraction. I was paranoid that they weren't going to let me into the delivery room, but they did. When they finally lifted Henry up out of her belly, I said, "Oh, my G-d!"

Wendy looked up at me and said, panicking, "What's wrong?"

"Nothing. He's really cute. He's perfect."

The umbilical cord was wrapped around his neck and at five pounds, fourteen ounces he seemed more like a doll than a baby. They handed him to me and I smiled at Wendy. She didn't look right. A nurse mentioned that she was hemorrhaging. I was quickly ushered out of the room with the baby. I sat in a little room outside delivery looking at Henry in the bassinet and thinking, What if something happens to Wendy? What will I do as a single mother? Would I even be able to keep this child? I wasn't the one who wanted kids in the first place. Plus, I had no legal rights to him yet. It was also a bit unnerving because here I was with this tiny baby and I knew nothing about babies. Nothing. I had never even changed a diaper. I felt alone and petrified.

Twenty minutes later, the nurse came out and told me that Wendy was going to be okay. I breathed another sigh of relief. The next day I went home and enlisted all my neighbors to help put Henry's room together. The crib was still in the box. With a little ingenuity (fueled by champagne), the room was ready for the prince's homecoming. Surrounded by our extended family, I felt like I had finally created my own version of *The Mary Tyler Moore Show*.

> "I look up to Ruth. Ruth was a really heroic woman. She left her family and came to a strange land. She was a wonderful daughter-in-law. She took care of her mother-in-law, nurtured her, and never left her. I was particularly fond of my mother-in-law. One of the saddest days in my life was when she became very sick. It was terrible watching someone who was so bright and so full of life deteriorate mentally and physically. The last five years of her life were difficult for me. I think I was a wonderful daughter-in-law. In some ways, I tried to be like Ruth."
>
> (Mother of four, homemaker, ultra Orthodox)

As excited as Sy and Marjorie were about Henry's birth, it took my own mother a while to realize that Henry was her grandchild. She certainly wasn't open about him to her friends. It's not like she sent out an announcement to all her friends . . .

MY DAUGHTER'S ROOMMATE OF TWELVE YEARS
AND DONOR NUMBER 6173
PROUDLY ANNOUNCE THE BIRTH OF THEIR SON
HENRY JACOB CALLAHAN GOLD.
HOW I AM RELATED TO HIM IS BEYOND ME.

A couple of days after Henry's birth, we went to get yarmulkes for his bris. I'll never forget how uncomfortable Wendy was after that C-section. She had so many stitches and hadn't left the house for six days. I put Henry in the Snugli—you know, the thing where you wear the baby and then you trip and fall and the baby dies. It took about forty-five minutes to walk the four blocks to the Judaica store. Wendy was in terrible pain; she was leaning on the counter by the cash register trying to hold herself up as I got in line to pay. I had the baby and the yarmulkes, and this woman came over to me and said, "Oh, my God! That baby is sooo cute. Florence, come here and take a look."

Her friend Florence walked over. "How adorable. How old is he?"

I responded, "Six days."

"What! Six days old? So precious." Then she took a good long look at me and said, "And *you*! Well, you look *fabulous*."

I said politely, "Thank you."

With that, I received the dirtiest look I'd ever seen from Wendy. I paid for the yarmulkes and we walked outside to Broadway, whereupon Wendy looked over at me and muttered, "Fuck you, you fucking bitch!"

I must admit that I deserved it. I really didn't know how painful childbirth was until I experienced it myself. Whenever anyone sees me with both kids and asks which pregnancy was harder, the first or the second? I always say, "Oh, the first one was a breeze. I didn't even gain any weight."

Along with her friend, and now our friend, Anna Switzer, Marjorie arranged Henry's bris. Phil Sherman, then mohel to the stars, officiated. It was a very small affair. Sy held Henry, and Phil did an amazing job. (Thank G-d.) He announced that Henry was named after his two grandfathers, Harold Gold and Jacob Walper.

As I held Henry during his bris, with not a member of my biological family in sight, I thought of my late father and how he would never know his namesake. It would take months for my mother to accept Henry and a couple of years to tell her friends about him. When he began to call her "Grandma," I said, "You have to start telling your friends or I won't let you see him anymore." I wondered if things would have been less difficult had my father still been alive. I honestly don't know how he would've reacted, but I cannot imagine him ever turning his back on something that meant so much to me. I hoped that this tiny baby would live up to his namesake. I hoped he would have his intellect and benevolence.

8

Who did you name your children after and why?

"Well, just between us, my daughter Linda is really named after my aunt Elaine. My husband thinks she's named after his mother."

AN ORTHODOX MOTHER OF TWO adult daughters whispered this while her husband walked past us to get a piece of cake from the kitchen. For most of the women, the naming of their children was not any big secret, but naming children, especially for Jews, is a loaded issue. This is primarily because children are named after the dead.

One woman we interviewed was someone I had met on a panel about Jewish women at the 92nd Street Y in New York. A development director of a prominent arts organization, she dressed the part in a tasteful black knit two-piece suit. Her jewelry was understated. There was an air of assurance and success about her. She showed us into an enormous conference room, where she had her assistant bring us cold drinks. I could tell Kate was thinking, We're not going to get anything. This is going to be a waste.

Before the door shut, before we took a sip of our sodas, she told us apropos of nothing that her mother was a Holocaust survivor and that her sister was mentally ill. Kate sat up and turned on the handheld tape recorder. We quickly realized that this woman was haunted by her mother's experience. She was terribly afraid that somehow, some way, she would damage her own children the way she had been damaged by her mother. It was a fear that we found was common among many children of Holocaust survivors. This fear seemed to manifest itself with this woman when she was about to get married.

"Before we were married, we had a prenuptial agreement. It was about naming our children. As a child I dreamed of naming my children after dead relatives, but there were so many of them I knew that I couldn't have that many children. It was a struggle all my life as to who was going to be the winner of this contest. Before we got married, we had a lot of therapeutic hours about having children. My husband said that my desire to name our future children after dead relatives wasn't really speaking to the happier parts of me. So we decided to name our children after people who lived a long and happy life. When Rachel was born, she was named after my mother's grandfather, Reuben. He

lived until almost one hundred and he died before the Holocaust. So there was a lot of meaning in celebrating lineage and family by naming her that. And then Scott was named after Grandma Tilly. We were searching for a T name. I gave birth in March and she had died the year before. We looked for T names—Taylor? Travis? Jews don't name their kids that. So we spelled it with an extra t at the end for Tilly."

Yes, Jews name their children after their dead as a tribute, but also because in Judaism anything happy has to include at least a little misery. It really is a beautiful custom and quite a fluid one at that. You can use the same name, the same first letter, or just the Hebrew name. I always knew exactly where my name came from, and it gave my parents a reason to tell me about my mother's father and my mother's grandmother, for whom I was named. I hoped naming Henry after his grandfathers would give him the same sense of continuance and heritage.

"My daughter is named after Abby Aldrich Rockefeller because I worked at the Museum of Modern Art and the print room was named after her. She was a fantastic woman with an independent spirit."
(Mother of two, art dealer, Reform)

My father was a tall man with a huge beatific smile that took up most of his face. He had deep-set eyes that could not hide his emotions. He was the third child of four, and the only boy. He didn't talk about his father much, but he loved his mother. He was quiet and smart. Whenever I mention his name now, people who knew him always use the same word to describe him—a gentleman. He passed the bar exam before he was twenty-one (he had to wait until he turned twenty-one to practice). After putting himself through college, he went into the army. He was stationed in Bristol, England, where he met his British girlfriend, Joyce. She visited my parents many years later, when they were all in their sixties. Afterward, my mother would say to anyone who would listen, "It's not any wife who would have the ex-girlfriend over for dinner."

My father loved theater, music, and gardening. We used to watch variety shows and beauty pageants together. When I asked my mother if he had had any hobbies that I didn't know about, she said, "Hobbies? He had one hobby— WORK!" He was a tax attorney and worked for the state of New Jersey. He always wore a suit and tie. To this day, I can hear the sound of his adding machine. He worked nonstop. And when he wasn't working, he would take naps. I was his sidekick. During the holidays we loved driving around looking at the Christmas lights. For some reason, he also loved Christmas carols. He would sing them all year round. But his favorite holiday was Halloween. (Being suburban Conservative Jews, we celebrated Halloween. Most Orthodox Jews do not. Why? Because it's a saint's day.) My father would purposely buy way too much candy to hand out to the trick-or-treaters. Then he would number the bags in the order in which we were supposed to give out the candy. The high-number bags were always filled with his favorite candies. He loved those Goldenberg Peanut Chews. (I can feel the fillings coming out of my teeth right now.) He was also always hiding candy—M&M's, Hershey's Kisses, and Canada Mints—throughout the house.

While the world was exploding with Vietnam, bell-bottoms, and psychedelic drugs, my father would come home every night at 5:45 on the dot, and we would all sit down to dinner at 6:00 sharp. Imagine a Jewish version of *Father Knows Best* crossed with *Diary of a Mad Housewife* and you'll have an idea of what it was like to grow up in the Gold house. Although my father seemed from another age, he never favored his son over his daughters, and I loved him for that.

Ironically, the one thing that was missing from my father was a good heart. He had his first massive heart attack when I was four and his second when I was twenty-seven. The morning he died, he had walked three miles and then he and my mother had lunch. In the afternoon, they went to the swim club. He swam ten laps and got out. As he was drying himself off, my mother was reaching down for her magazine, when she heard a noise. She looked up to see my father collapsing. The ambulance came and the paramedics revived him. I was at home in NYC. I had just gotten back to my apartment after the gym when my sister stopped by unexpectedly to say hello on the way to a class she was taking. I walked into the other room and there was a message on the answering machine. It was my mother saying in a very calm voice, "Judith, I'm at Rahway hospital. I think your father had a heart attack. You might want to come."

When we arrived, my father was in the ICU. I saw my mother sitting there wearing her bathing suit and a terry-cloth wrap. Right then, I realized how, in a moment, life can change. One minute she was reaching for a magazine, and the next, the man she'd depended on for so many years is in a coma. That night, I went to the swim club and drove my father's navy blue Buick Century home. I still have his car keys.

He remained on a life support system for six days, until we finally convinced the doctors to unplug him. He died twenty-three hours later with all of us at his bedside. My sister hadn't gone into his room for days because the sound of the life support system was so disturbing to her. After he was unplugged, my brother asked my sister to come back into the room. He told her it was quiet now, that he was breathing on his own. It was as if my father knew, as if he had waited until we were all there before he took his last breath. At that moment we all said Psalm 27 aloud. That was the hardest room I've ever had to leave.

> *"I wanted to name my third daughter Rina, which means happy. My father-in law came to the hospital and he asked me to name her after his late wife. I was stunned. I had very bad feelings about my mother-in-law. But how could I refuse him? He was a good father-in-law. So I said yes. And the interesting thing is that this daughter turned out to be the sweetest and nicest person that everyone loves. She is very special and I always said that G-d compensated me for doing something that I really did not want to do, but did out of respect."*
>
> (Mother of three, librarian, Conservative)

It's always a tricky thing naming a baby. I respected what this woman did, and I could understand her agony in naming her daughter after her mother-in-law, a woman she did not like. She told us that when her own mother saw how great her father-in-law was, she said, "He is the cream in your coffee."

My own father taught me one of the most important lessons of my life after he died. At the funeral one of his friends came up to me and said, "You know, several years ago when I also had a heart attack, it was tax season and I didn't know what to do. I was about to lose all my clients and then your father visited me in the hospital. He told me not to worry about anything. He filed extensions for all of my clients, and every weekend he came over and did their returns for me. Never asked for a penny. He saved my business."

That day I made a vow to myself that I would use whatever talents I had to help others. Whenever anyone asks me to do a benefit and I am free, I say yes. And I have to say, I enjoy those performances the most.

I think about my father every day. On the fifteenth anniversary of his death, I found myself at the computer, jotting down a couple of things I remembered and learned from my father. This was the list:

- Nothing worth anything comes easy.
- Do what you love.
- Love what you do.
- There's nothing like picking your own fruit off of a tree.
- When you yell at the sprinkler, it doesn't yell back.
- Make sure you plan out every minute of your vacations.
- When you do something nice for someone, don't talk about it.
- Always wear a shirt in public.
- Everyone hates the Jews.

- Family is the most important thing in the whole world.
- Watching a rosebush grow from a seed is beautiful.
- Be very careful whom you let into your heart.
- Read a lot.
- Take naps.
- Exercise.
- Don't waste time—there's not a lot of it.
- Always try to guess who's going to win the Miss America Pageant.
- Hide your favorite candy.
- You can have a bad temper and still be a good person.
- Men don't necessarily have to drink beer and love sports.
- There's nothing like getting dressed up in your favorite outfit.
- Never eat dinner alone.

I dream about him all of the time. I tell him what is going on and what the boys are up to. Even after so many years, it's hard to accept my father's death. I wish he had met Henry and Ben. I am sure he would have gotten a kick out of them. Whenever it's Halloween, I always tell Henry to give away the crappy candy first.

9

How important is it for your children and/or grandchildren to be raised Jewish?

"Before I met my husband, I dated someone very seriously who was Catholic. And I know firsthand that there's a different way of looking at things. Because of that experience, I think I would find it harder to relate to my children if they married someone non-Jewish and raised their children Christian. It would be very hard not to have that common thread."

A MODERN ORTHODOX MOTHER OF THREE TOLD US THIS while her young boys ran around with New York Yankee yarmulkes planted firmly on their heads. It made me wonder if she wished her Christian boyfriend had been Jewish or if she would have broken up with him anyway.

Most Jewish children are told that they must marry someone Jewish. And when that doesn't happen, they are told that they must raise any future children Jewish. When that doesn't happen, the parents ask if they can come over to light the menorah on Chanukah. When that doesn't happen, they sit in the corner with pusses on their faces, glaring at the dreidel ornament on the "holiday tree."

For Kate the choice to raise her son Jewish after being raised Catholic herself was not a difficult one. "My partner, Laurie, the biological mother, is Jewish—therefore, he is Jewish." (That's how it was with Wendy. Her mother was Jewish and her father Irish Catholic.) But Kate draws the line at converting. "When you believe that the Messiah has arrived, it's kind of hard to go back to waiting." After her son Timothy started Hebrew school, I got a rather irate phone call from her.

"Jude, is every holiday about surviving some massacre?" Kate shouted, exasperated. "Your religion is like too depressing dot com."

"We have happy holidays," I said defensively. "There's Chanukah."

"Yeah, there's a nice drawing of Judah Maccabee pummeling the Greeks on the Sub-Zero."

"Well, what about Passover? It's a celebration." Damn, I regretted using Passover as an example immediately.

"It's like the prequel to *Silence of the Lambs*. Next." Kate was winning.

"There's Purim. That's fun." What could be wrong with Purim? I thought.

"Haman gets murdered," Kate answered. "It's a *Sopranos* episode in 50 B.C. FYI, I love that Tisha B'av, the catchall holiday in case some massacre was forgotten."

"Well, Kate, your religion is not always happy. What about Easter?" Her religion wasn't all Santa Claus and Easter Bunnies. I saw the trailer for *The Passion of the Christ*.

"Wrong. Jesus gets crucified and then he comes back to life. It's happy. Jude, just face it, in a nutshell your religion is 'They attacked us, we beat them, let's eat.'" G-d, I hate it when Kate steals my lines.

"Wait, I've got it, Lag B'Omer," I shouted, sending my earpiece flying.

"Lay what? What the hell is that?" Kate said, incredulous.

"Birthday of the trees."

"The birthday of the what? Christ, that's it. I'm calling Tom Cruise and signing up."

"Go right ahead, MELanie Gibson. Go right ahead," I yelled, as I did my victory dance.

A Catholic mother trying to raise a Jewish child isn't as unique as you might think. And there are more and more

Jewish children who were not born Jewish. We interviewed a successful movie producer from Los Angeles who was in New York promoting her latest blockbuster. Her five-year-old was with one of her "G-d mums," so she had an hour of respite from work and motherhood. From her black high-top sneakers to her surfer T-shirt, she dressed more like a teenaged boy than a high-powered LA type. With blond curly hair clipped close to the scalp, her one concession to glamour was a series of diamonds that studded her left ear.

"The decision to adopt Talia came rather quickly. I called my parents and they both got on the line and I told them. My mother was very supportive. My father really resisted. He said to me, 'Why would you want to do that, you have the perfect life.' And I said, 'Look, I am not getting younger; it is important to me that there's more to life than just me. I don't want to be one of those self-involved gay people spending all of my money on myself.' Then my father said, 'Well, it's not like you're adopting a Chinese or black baby.' And then I said, 'Well, actually the baby is biracial. She's half-black.' He went crazy and hung up the phone on me. He didn't talk to me for three weeks. My mother came down to help me the day Talia was born. A couple of days later, I got a call from my father. 'Your mother said the baby is fantastic.' And then he apologized. He asked me when the baby naming would be and said that he would be there for that.

True to his word, my father came to Talia's baby naming, and once he met her it was love at first sight."

When Henry was almost one month old, I got a job on *The Rosie O'Donnell Show* as a writer and producer. I had known Rosie for years from the comedy circuit. When she offered me a job, I jumped at it. I didn't want to travel anymore. I wanted to be around for Henry. It was hard, though, because I'd always thought of myself as a performer, but now I was a mother and Henry came first. This is not to say that the job was any easier than being on the road. For some insane reason, I was training for the marathon, so I would get up at 5 A.M. and then would head over to the studio by 7:00 and have my jokes written by 7:45 because it was a live show. I would get home at around 6 or 7 P.M., which was considered early by many of the producers. By the time I got home, I was so exhausted, all I wanted to do was sleep, but Henry never, ever slept. He was up every fifteen minutes. And I refused to get up with him. I used to say to Wendy, "Why should we both be tired?" which would set off an attack of SARS (sudden angry response syndrome). She got me back, though. After I had Ben, *she* refused to get up.

"We moved four years ago from Switzerland when my husband was transferred for business. And the first day I moved here

to New Jersey, I just loved it. Everybody is
proud to be Jewish here. And I have the
opportunity to give my kids a Jewish day
school. In Switzerland, we were always hiding
ourselves. We were never proud to say, 'I'm
Jewish.' I never told my friends that I was
keeping kosher. I used to say I'm a vegetarian.
But here I can keep kosher. I can raise my
children Jewish. And I can be proud of it."
(Mother of two, jeweler, Modern Orthodox)

However exhausting new parenthood and the job was, I
loved working for *The Rosie O'Donnell Show*. One of my favorite moments on the show was when Madonna was a
guest. She had just had her daughter Lourdes, and there
was a rumor that she was going to come on with her. One
of the producers asked me if I would bring Henry in as the
"fake baby." I was all high and mighty, saying, "There is no
way my child is going into show business." (If I had known
then how much kids cost, I would have had them earning
their Pampers before the cord was cut.) But back then I still
had ideas on how to raise a child. Wendy had no such
qualms; she was, like, "Oh, my God, we can put it in his
baby book" (which is the size of the OED).

So the day of, I met Wendy and Henry downstairs at
eight-thirty to bring them up. There were photographers

everywhere. They all assumed Wendy was Madonna's nanny and started pushing to get a photo. It got scary, and Wendy started shouting that she was going to drop Henry. He was only a month or so old at the time. Instinctively, I wrapped my arms around both of them, and we pushed our way into the elevator. Then the photographers started following us in and I pushed them back. For a moment I understood why movie stars have such a love/hate relationship with the press. We got into the studio unscathed. Madonna was backstage, and we introduced her to Henry. She told us how cute he was and I told her that he loves music. While she was waiting to go on, Henry began to get restless and Madonna began to sing to him and he began to scream. Then she walked on with Henry, and the audience went ballistic thinking that she had brought Lourdes. Rosie said to Madonna, "That baby is adorable, but it's not yours." Madonna grinned and fessed up. And then I came on stage to pick up Henry, and that was his brief foray into superstardom. The next day the cover of the New York *Post* had a picture of Madonna holding Henry, and the headline read, "Oh! Henry!" Then, my mother called.

"I just got about twenty calls asking me if Henry was your son. They saw you grab him from Madonna on the Rosie show."

And I was, like, "So what did you say?"

"I told them the truth."

"Version 5.1 or did a later one come out?"

"Don't be so fresh. I told them that your roommate had a baby and you adopted him."

"She's not my roommate, Mom. She's my . . ." And before I could get out the word "partner," my mother screamed, "WHATEVER. They know what I mean."

How could they? Did her friends think that some cad had knocked up Wendy, and that since I was splitting the rent I figured I might as well pay for half of the baby, too?

Then my sister called, and she was, like, "I don't know why you have to bring him outside and parade him around like that. All my friends were asking why they said it was your baby."

"Umh, that's because it is my baby."

"WHATEVER," my sister said as she slammed down the phone.

What was it going to take, I wondered, for my family to accept this child?

"There is no question. They must be raised Jewish."
(Mother of four, administrative assistant, Conservative)

Working for the Rosie show was fun, because I never knew who I was going to meet. We had a kid on who was obsessed with vacuum cleaners, and a cabdriver who gave all of his customers a piece of gum for the ride. My favorite one was a thirteen-year-old girl who won the Scripps National Spelling Bee, Rebecca Sealfon. She had successfully spelled—or rather, energetically shouted—the word "eponym," which I have since found out is by definition the name of a person, whether real or fictitious, that has given rise to the name of a particular place, tribe, discovery, or other item. Because of her rather unique spelling style, which was pause, scream, jump, pause, scream, jump, every television program around the country wanted her on. I knew she was Jewish and that she was home-schooled. So I played the *Shabbos* card—I called her family at home and left a message. I told them who I was and why I would like to have Rebecca on the show. It was a Friday, and I asked if they could please call me before sundown.

I got a call back within an hour. I needed to assure Rebecca's mother that we did not want to make fun of her at all, but rather wanted to celebrate her uniqueness. I told them I knew what it was like to be the odd girl out and an easy target. Rebecca was booked that following Monday. She was the greatest guest. The audience *loved* her! The following year she became our on-air correspondent for the spelling bee. That same year we won our first Emmy, at Radio City Music Hall. Watching Rebecca's excitement at having been singled out by us led me to wish someone had made me feel special when I was home alone every afternoon after school. Somehow by helping her, I had helped exorcise my own childhood demons of being the gawky tall misfit.

And although things with Wendy were not great—we were both exhausted; I was working a "real job" and she had a bit of postpartum blues—we were moving forward. Our apartment, however, which had seemed so huge when we first moved in, seemed to shrink as Henry grew. Wendy, ever the interior decorator, would bring in one Israeli contractor after another to try to expand its dimensions. One time I overheard one of them say, "How tall are the people upstairs?" Wendy said, "Short." "Good, we'll raise the ceiling and make this apartment a duplex."

No one ever told us how much stuff a kid needs. Jews usually don't have baby showers before the baby is born. (It's based on old superstitions that usually involve spitting into the air and saying "*poo poo poo*.") Instead, they have the UPS man who comes every day for a year after the baby is born. And the UPS man brought our bundle of joy such things as: the Gymini Exersaucer, the complete collection of Baby Einstein videos (someone really stoned must have created them), a wall jumper, a walker, a Boppy, a Babybjörn, the Prima Pappa chair, the Pack and Play (so I could put him down and ignore him), the Tot Lok system (to keep him away from my Ambien—I don't share well), a bottle washer, 264-count boxes of diapers, aloe wipes, the porpoise singing family for the bath, a baby mobile (looks like it was designed by B. F. Skinner), the complete library written by Tanya Hoban (the Tolstoy for the nonverbal set), a whoozit (which I renamed a whazzit), a kick 'n play (let's teach them to be aggressive now), an Intellitable (they stand, they press buttons, it sounds like a Philip Glass composition— yes, that bad), a Floppy baby (please give it an exoskeleton), the Little People Discovery City (they're sort of like munchkins in *The Wizard of Oz* except they all hold menial jobs), a Lamaze rattle play system (as a rule I stay away from anything named Lamaze), the Sassy stacking cups (how about just a set of measuring cups and save the $20?). People convince you that unless your infant has these things and uses these things, he'll never get into nursery school. And in Manhattan, I have to say (having gone through the process), they may be right.

As Henry began to grow and thrive, I started to think about what sort of Jewish traditions I wanted to pass on to him besides guilt, OCD, and feelings of inadequacy.

Although I knew I wanted to impart the traditions that I had grown up with, I was conflicted about how religious I wanted to be. But, the truth is, I did become more religious once I started having children, and I wondered if other women felt the same way. And one of the things I began thinking about was keeping kosher again.

#10

Are you kosher?

"Only in the house. The kids don't know that."

A SHY WOMAN IN HER EARLY FORTIES confided this, while making sure none of her friends heard. Kosher (or kashrut) are the laws Jews have about foods that can and cannot be eaten. For example, we're not supposed to eat shellfish or pork. So don't send the Hershowitzs a five-pound platter of bacon-wrapped shrimp for Chanukah. Jewish law also determines how the animal should be slaughtered and how the meat should be prepared before it's consumed. Jews who keep kosher usually observe Shabbat. My mother always kept the Sabbath (Shabbat), and every Friday night we said our prayers, ate our challah and chicken, and went to shul. I dreaded it, except after services they always had really delicious brownies. The roots of Shabbat can be found in the Bible. After God created the Earth, he stopped work on the seventh day and rested. Shabbat is the designated day of rest, prayer, and reflection. It starts on Friday at sundown. Every Friday, the *New York Times* always prints the exact time of sundown on the front page. It reads, "Jewish women and girls light your candles at . . ."

> "In Orthodox circles there are two types of Jews. There are the ffb's, the frum from birth, and the bt's, bat shuva. My husband grew up in a non-Orthodox, non-observant home. And there was a time when I got to college I thought to myself, I really don't want to be Jewish anymore. When my husband and I first got married, we were students and poor. We'd go to Tony Roma's and chow down on ribs or the ground round. We weren't kosher for a number of years, and then we had children. We knew we had to get serious. We began to think, How do we want our children to grow up? I got back to being observant, and we have been kosher ever since."
>
> (Mother of three, CEO, Modern Orthodox)

Shabbat ends on Saturday at sundown. It is considered by observant Jews to be the most sacred ritual in the Jewish religion. Before kids, I would occasionally observe Shabbat. We would go over to the Cohens' for Shabbat when we were invited, and soon they started setting two extra places for Wendy and me every Friday night. I realized how amazing this tradition really was. We all sat around eating, drinking, and talking about our week. There was no TV, no place to go. Just uninterrupted family time with friends popping by for dessert or a glass of wine.

After Henry was born, I decided I would not work on Friday nights unless it was absolutely necessary. I couldn't wait until the end of the work week. It's amazing when you hear your kids say, "Is today Friday? It's *Shabbos*? YEAH!!!" With all the chaos of bringing up kids in NYC, it's nice to look forward to some downtime. It's a time for remembering who is no longer there. My good friend and fellow comic Carol Henry succumbed to AIDS in 1992, four years before Henry was born. The cruel irony was that the life-saving drug cocktail was only two years away. After the boys were born, Carol's mother, Anne, sent each one a kiddush cup. On Fridays when I see them raise their cups, I think of Carol and how cruel life is sometimes, and how it's still hard after all these years.

Marjorie readily admits that keeping kosher and observing the Sabbath is in itself a challenge.

"It's so difficult being a nonreligious person married to an Orthodox man, because religion carries all these rules with it. Take

Friday sundown to Saturday sundown. Shabbat. How hard can that be, you're asking me? Twenty-four hours? Well, imagine that for twenty-four hours, you can't talk on the phone. You can't turn on the light. You can't drive. You can't watch TV. You can't handle money. You can't ride on an elevator. You can ride on an elevator—but you can't press the button—so you hint. 'Oh, I wonder what floor I live on? What's the number of children I have times two?' In my building people think I have selective Saturday Alzheimer's. I keep telling myself that I keep a kosher home for the girls, but they're grown and out of the house now. Sometimes just before sundown on a Friday, I close my eyes and dream about going to Red Lobster and ordering the surf and turf."

(Mother of two, head of not-for-profit agency, confused)

I grew up kosher, and I cannot tell you how many times I would come into the kitchen to see my mother clutching a utensil, sobbing. It was always the same wrenching cry: "Oh, my G-d! Who put this knife in this drawer? Why is the meat knife in the dairy drawer?! I try so hard and look what she does! It's the girl. The girl did it." "The girl"—that horrible sobriquet given to the cleaning woman who straightened up our bedrooms for us. My mother was always blaming things on her.

Jews who keep kosher separate meat from dairy. We can't eat a cheeseburger—well, you can if you want to go to hell. (And it's worth it. Gorgonzola with fried onions.) We also have different plates, pots and pans, and utensils for meat and dairy. Now, if you make a mistake, say you use a meat spoon for ice cream, you have to purify it by burying it in the earth for three days. So whenever "the girl" had inadvertently made the mistake of mixing up the silver, my mother would yell, "JUDITH, get me the plant. GET ME THE PLANT!" Jews can re-kosher their silverware either by boiling it or by sticking it in the earth for three days, and in our case "the earth" was houseplants. Whenever I set the table for dinner, it was ferns to the left of the plate, roses and violets to the right.

"Am I what? Umh, no."
(Mother of one, real estate agent, Reform)

Before we had kids I would change the plates and silverware over for Passover. But as time went on, it just felt wrong not having a kosher kitchen, and Wendy saw it as an opportunity to feed her shopping habit. She went to Bloomingdale's and bought new plates and dishes. And then the next thing I knew the Israeli contractor man was redoing the kitchen.

The birth of Henry made me become a more observant Jew, but it also raised a lot of the conflicts that I had with Judaism. Most notably, I had a problem with the separation between men and women in shul, because one of my favorite memories from when I was a child is sitting next to my father in shul looking at the memorial plaques and watching the light from an open window envelop us. I'd run my fingers through the fringes of his prayer shawl while listening to him recite his prayers.

#11

What do you think of men and women being separated at shul?

"It doesn't really bother me. First of all, I don't go to the synagogue as much as my husband. So I do not want him sitting next to another woman. And secondly, if I sat with a man, I couldn't notice the nice hat the woman next to me was wearing."

MANY OF THE WOMEN WE INTERVIEWED, INCLUDING THE one above, liked sitting separately from their husbands at shul. It gave them a chance to visit with their friends. Were there any women out there who felt as I did?

Kate skis in Park City, Utah, so she was able to interview some Jewish mothers out there. Many of the present-day Jewish families have lived there for generations. Most arrived in the 1820s as fur trappers and merchants cashing in on the

California Gold Rush. But now many are new transplants from the East lured by the fantastic skiing. When Kate got home, she came over and pulled out the tape recorder. "Listen to what this woman said when I asked her if men and women should be separated at shul."

"When I was a little girl in Massachusetts, I would go to shul with my grandfather on Saturday. No one else from my family came. My parents weren't religious. My grandfather was Orthodox. I loved my grandfather. He was kind and soft-spoken. When we got to shul, he let go of my hand, and I would climb the stairs to the balcony to sit with the women and the children. I hated sitting there. The women were so loud; too loud—I couldn't hear the rabbi. I would see my grandfather swaying and saying his prayers. And I would dream that I was an angel. That I had wings and I could fly down below to the men. And somehow, at the end of the service, I would wind up at my grandfather's elbow. He would wrap me under his prayer shawl and hide me. And for the rest of the service we were together."
(Mother of one, writer, nonpracticing)

At shul I always sat between my father and mother. My mother always wore special jewelry for shul. I used to call it the family jewels. This ring was from my great aunt, the bracelet from my grandmother. On those long Saturday and holiday mornings at shul, when I'd measure my hands against my father's, he made me feel what no one else could—little and safe. I did not find myself in an Orthodox synagogue until my father died. It was an odd experience. I went to say the mourner's kaddish, which is said during the first twelve months after a loved one's death. Although it was an incredibly painful thing to do, I needed to feel my father near me once again.

When I was on the road, I would look synagogues up in the phone book. Some of them were Orthodox. At the first one I went to, I followed the crowd inside, and one of the men stopped me and pointed upstairs. Disoriented, I climbed the steps and found a seat among the women and children. I looked at the gallery below and saw the boys and men. Then I closed my eyes and said kaddish for my father. The wonderful thing about kaddish is that the word "dead" is not mentioned once. It is prayer about G-d, goodness, and greatness. It is also a prayer of peace. This is an English translation of the kaddish:

Magnified and sanctified be God's great name in the world which He has created according to His will. May He establish His kingdom soon, in our lifetime. Let us say: Amen.

May His great name be praised to all eternity.

Hallowed and honored, extolled and exalted, adored and acclaimed be the name of the Holy One, though He is above all the praises, hymns, and songs of adoration which men can utter. Let us say: Amen.

May God grant abundant peace and life to us and to all Israel. Let us say: Amen.

May He who ordains harmony in the universe grant peace to us and to all Israel. Let us say: Amen.

When I closed my eyes and began the mourner's kaddish, I did not care where I was at that point, but when I finished, I looked down into the gallery and saw the men and boys sitting together and I thought about how lucky those boys were that they got to sit with their dads.

We met one woman, a psychiatrist whose husband insisted that they switch to an Orthodox shul after years of going to a Conservative one. They did, she explained, so their girls would attend the same shul as their friends from school. But this decision created great friction between her and her husband. When we asked this question, her tone alternated pain and downright anger. A mother of two teenaged girls, she had come from work. Dressed in a conservative blue suit, her green eyes were offset by her short auburn hair. She took a long sip of red wine before she answered the question.

"That's a very hot topic in our house. In the last few years we have joined an Orthodox temple, and for lots of reasons, I find it very disconcerting. I understand what they say the differences are between men and women and how the role of the women is integral to Judaism. But on both an emotional and spiritual level I feel relegated to a different status."

Sometimes on Saturday, I let Sy take Henry and Ben to his shul. He treats my two boys like the sons he never had. I like to watch them walk there together, the three of them—Sy with his prayer shawl and the kids in their yarmulkes. It's like a scene from *Fiddler on the Roof*. I think if Sy starred as Tevye in the Upper West Side version, it would go something like this:

Two mommies and no dad
Sounds crazy, no?
But in our little village
called the Upper West Side

you might say every one of us
is a little meshuga
trying to get a bagel and
a smear from Zabar's
without getting slammed by a
baby stroller
It isn't easy
You may ask why
do we stay up here
where it is so crowded?
That I can tell you in two words—
we stay here because on the Upper
West Side
There is RENT CONTROL

In Sy's shul they separate the men and the women with barbed wire and attack dogs. Marjorie refuses to go. She finds it insulting. I don't let Henry and Ben go too often, because I don't want them growing up thinking of women as second-class citizens.

One time, Sy invited me to come along with my boys. I watched Sy and my kids walk through the front door, and as I was about to follow them, his daughter Lucy grabbed me and motioned for me to follow her. She pulled open a gate and led me through an alley. I ran down the steps into the separate entrance, playing an elaborate game of hopscotch to avoid the rodents scurrying out of a ripped-open bag of garbage. Lucy pulled opened the door to the basement of the brownstone, revealing the women sitting on metal folding chairs. Ten feet and a fence separated them from where the men stood with an unobstructed view of the rabbi and his pulpit. Henry ran back and forth between the women and men while pointing at me and shouting in an annoying singsong voice, "Ha, ha, you can't sit there. I can! Bye!" Needless to say, it was a long time before I went back.

At B'nai Jeshurun, the synagogue I joined on the Upper West Side, the boys sit next to me, and it's a lot more intimate and inviting. There's music, something we never had in our synagogue growing up. Henry and Ben bring their instruments and play along. They dance and run around, and when they get tired they plop themselves in my lap.

But as foreign as it is for me to sit separately from the men, for many of the women we interviewed it's the only way they've ever known.

> "I grew up like that. It wouldn't be fair for me to answer because I've never done it any other way. I like sitting with the girls. I have two daughters so I always have them with me."
> (Mother of two, homemaker, Modern Orthodox)

That woman gave me pause. I had never thought about it as a bonding experience between a mother and her daughters. I don't have girls, however, and the thought of being separated from my children simply because they are boys makes me sad. I have such fond memories of sitting in shul between both my parents as a child. It is my greatest hope that when my boys grow into men with families of their own, they will sit with their wives and their daughters beside them, playing with the fringes of their tallis.

#12

Do you find Judaism limiting or empowering?

"There is a saying, the man is the head of the household, but the woman is the neck. It's really very true, because in a traditional Jewish home, the mother rules; no ifs, ands, or buts." (Mother of three, CEO, Orthodox)

THIS IS A WIDELY ACCEPTED SAYING, BUT I ALWAYS FOUND it sort of an old-fashioned cop-out. As I grew up, I noticed that my brother had more freedom than I did. It exasperated me. "Why does HE get to do that?!?!" I especially hated that at the Passover seder my father and my brother both got pillows for their chairs because a man is supposed to recline. What about me? I need to recline, too! I grew up Conservative, or rather, Conservadox. Women weren't allowed to open the ark where the Torah was held, and they weren't allowed to hold the Torah. I used to ask my mother, "Why can't I open the ark?", "Why can't I hold the Torah?"

I used to see little boys doing what I wasn't allowed to do, and I'd get irate at the injustice of it all. Now, you would think my mother would agree with me—after all, she was the only girl in her Hebrew school—but all she could say was "Men and women have different roles, Judith."

In the Torah, women have three mandates to uphold. Men have 613 strings on their prayer shawl/tallis, symbolizing the 613 commandments they are required to observe. Women are given a lighter load, so they will be free to focus on home and family. Their three mandates are:

- Lighting the candles on the Sabbath.
- Taking dough from a small batch of everything you bake and setting it aside as a temple offering. (Store-bought kosher-baked goods explicitly say that this has been done, so you can enjoy them without guilt. Oh, the guilt.)
- Taking the ritual bath after that time of the month.

The three mandates my mother observed were:

- Make sure your kids know how miserable they are making you.
- Make sure your kids go to college and marry Jews.
- Make sure your kids know how miserable they are making you.

One mother of two told us that she had grown up in a conservative family on the Upper West Side. When she came out as a lesbian to her family, they were at first angry and confused, but eventually they accepted their daughter. They were more upset, however, by how dismissive their daughter was of her Jewish heritage. Why couldn't she be gay and still be a Jew? they asked her time and time again. Her attitude changed when she met her partner, Jane, whom she wanted to marry. She quickly found that there weren't any rabbis who would do a commitment or marriage ceremony between a Jew and non-Jew. And to her surprise Jane agreed to convert.

> *"I had always found it limiting, and for a while, when I was first coming out, I rejected Judaism and I didn't think it had a place for me. Then recently, because of Jane's process of conversion, I started to study and learn more, and I have found it very empowering."*

Although I let the boys go to Sy's synagogue, I also make sure they come to ours more often. It's imperative for me to have them see how important it is to me for us to sit as a family and to see women in positions of leadership within the synagogue. A woman rabbi speaking from the bimah ensures that I will never have to answer the question "Why can't girls do that?" And during Passover, *all* of us get to recline.

"I never felt like Judaism was oppressing me or that I was a second-class citizen."
(Mother of two, lawyer, Conservative)

As Henry began to get older, Wendy and I began to talk about giving him a sibling. By this time, we were like every other old married couple on the Upper West Side. We both worked (albeit different hours), we had *Shabbos* every Friday night, we made playdates, and we were both generally exhausted. There was rarely time for date night, and, boy, are children expensive! We focused our lives around our child and our careers. We made lots of new friends because of Henry's day care, but we would argue—a lot. I think we were both frustrated by the lack of intimacy combined with our perpetual exhaustion. We had different interests. I always wanted to exercise and play basketball with Henry, and Wendy loved to decorate and shop shop shop. I would often wake up in the morning and see the computer on and the credit card beside it, and I knew a big box of something was on its way. Her spending made me nervous, but somehow Wendy could justify the necessity of each and every purchase.

Henry's friends started getting siblings, and he desperately wanted a little sister. Wendy and I had always agreed that she would have the first child and I would have the second. Boy or girl, I knew that if we were going to have another baby, I would need to do it soon. I had turned thirty-seven, and I wasn't getting any younger.

> "I think you let the role limit you as much as you want it to limit you. I don't feel like I need to go up with the Torah and carry it around. I believe that as women, we definitely contribute to the family in carrying on Judaism. Let's face it, men could do the job, but not as well."
>
> (Mother of four, teacher, Conservative)

Picking out a new donor and getting inseminated was kind of a weird out-of-body experience. I also remember thinking how bizarre it was that making this baby was such a solitary activity. Even though I had Wendy, I felt so alone. I didn't know if having another child would help or hurt my relationship with her. The funny thing was that we were good at being parents together, and I thought that was enough. I mean, everyone else seemed just as miserable and tired all of the time. It seemed to work out well that I was a night person and she was a morning person; she was great with babies and I was great as they got older. Plus, when she was shopping, decorating, and planning parties, I got to play outside!

I loved being a mother—much more than I had ever imagined I would.

The only thing I could not control was the sex of the baby. With a little help from my credit card and a fertility specialist, I waited for nature to take its course.

13

Did you raise your sons differently from your daughters?

"Unfortunately, I think I am a bit tougher on my son. I tell my daughter that she is pretty, but I never tell my son that he is handsome. My son wanted to wear dresses when he was a kid, and I tried to let him, but my husband would not allow it." (Mother of two, doctor, Conservative)

MY MOTHER ALSO ADMITS SHE TREATED HER SON DIFFER-ently from her daughters. She described her three children this way: "I would tell Alan not to do something and he would say okay and then do whatever he wanted. I would tell Jane not to do something and she would say okay and not even think of doing it. And I would tell Judith not to do something and she would do whatever she wanted and give me a big argument about it." When I was very young, my father sat down with my older brother and sister to explain about the birds and the bees. When he was finished, he pointed to my brother, Alan, and said, "You can do it before you're married." And then he pointed to Jane. "But you can't." My mother always said that there were certain things you allowed boys to do that you didn't allow girls. For my brother, Alan, it meant he didn't didn't have an egg timer attached to his belt.

> "When my son was born, I was overjoyed because he was a boy. And I said, Sandra, you should not think that way. Then when I had Danielle, I said, 'I am so happy it's a girl because now I have someone I can relate to.' In terms of treating them differently, well, to be quite honest, I do. I am much harder on my son because he's, quite frankly, and I hate to say, lazy."
> (Mother of three, social worker, Orthodox)

My mother always said that it would've been much easier to bring up children in the city. She grew up two blocks from where I live right now. But it's been a hard balance trying to give Henry some freedom while realizing we are not in the suburbs and he cannot bike to the neighbors'. I just started letting him walk to Hebrew school by himself so I can also put his newfound freedom to good use by having him run errands for me like dropping off the dry cleaning or picking up some coffee. Of course, he has his cell phone with him at all times so I can check up on him. I know there will come a time when he will take the subway by himself, or get his driver's license, and, of course, I am terrified. Would I let my daughter walk to Hebrew school by herself at the same age? I'd like to say yes, but I don't have a daughter, so I really don't know. I like to think that I am raising my sons differently from how I was raised. I try to expose them to all sorts of people. I have a house in Provincetown, and Henry knows all of the drag queens by name. He plays basketball with all of my friends (who needless to say are mostly women). I think because of the way he's grown up, he's not quick to judge people.

Recently, we were driving and Henry was playing with his Game Boy. He looked up and asked me, "Mommy, is your friend Jeanne a lesbian?" When I replied, "Yes," Henry said, "Oh," and he went back to playing with his Game Boy. Now, if I was nine years old and in the car with my mother and I asked, "Mom, is Mrs. Rosenbaum a lesbian?", we would've crashed into the divider on the Garden State Parkway. As scary as it was to be raised by one Jewish mother, I have to feel for my kids because they have two

Jewish mothers. Although, I'd like to think they will have a distinct advantage when they start dating. I can just see Henry trying to pick up some innocent girl by saying, "I totally understand women, after all, I have two moms."

"Yes, I raised my son very strictly. Everyone told me that I was too strict, so when I had my daughter I wasn't so strict. In retrospect, it should have been the other way around. My son is the light of my life. I know that sounds trite, but he really truly is."
(Mother of two, bookkeeper, Conservative)

I've tried to teach my boys to respect women and how important equality is between the sexes, although sometimes they do take the lessons too much to heart and my consciousness-raising backfires. A couple of years ago, we took both boys to a Reproductive Rights Freedom March in Washington, DC. It was a beautiful April day—-about sixty-five degrees and sunny—and we explained to the kids while we were marching that this was why our country was so great, because we had freedom of speech (for another month), and women had the right do what they needed to do with their bodies (for another day and a half). So we get home on Sunday evening feeling all patriotic and empowered, and the next morning Henry wakes up and he says at breakfast, "I wanna wear shorts today." Now, April in the Northeast is quite the precarious month weather-wise. It happened to be about thirty-seven degrees and raining that morning. I told Henry that he could not wear shorts to school. "I wanna wear shorts!" he declared. I told him, "You are not wearing shorts. It's thirty-seven degrees and raining and last week you had a fever. No way." Then the kicker came. He said to me, point-blank, "I went to Washington, DC, to march so that people wouldn't tell you what to do with your body and now you're telling me what I can wear on mine?" What the hell was I supposed to say to that? So he's been off the respirator for over a month now, which the doctor said is great.

It's funny—these days I feel more comfortable around little boys than little girls. I'd like to think that if I had daughters, I would yell and mistreat them regardless of their sex, but as the date for my CVS prenatal test drew near, I remember being nervous. What if it was a girl? I knew a lot about raising a boy, but a girl, what would she be like? Then I began to panic—what if she was like *me*? I immediately started to pray for a boy. And lo and behold my prayers were answered. Everyone says that sons love their mothers more—especially Jewish ones—and I needed someone who was going to change my diaper at the Hebrew Home for the Aged.

Many of the Orthodox women were quite adamant in

their belief that boys should be raised differently from girls. Having raised their children during the 1960s and the 1970s, they were of the firm belief that boys needed to be raised as good potential providers and girls as obedient wives, as they had been. As insular as their worlds were, however, it was hard to shield their daughters from the real world outside.

A Sephardic woman in her sixties seemed particularly mystified by the path her daughter had chosen. Wearing a conservatively styled wig, this mother of two adult children had on a beautiful violet wool tweed suit with a rich silk blouse that buttoned against her throat. By the way she dressed, we could tell outward appearances mattered to her very much. When we asked her if she raised her son and daughter differently, she shook her head as if she still could not believe the path that her daughter had taken. What had the daughter done? Had she become a drug addict? Had she married a non-Jew? Was she a lesbian? A stand-up comic? She took a sip of tea from a glass and began.

"Well, my daughter got ballet lessons. We took mother-and-daughter painting courses at the Museum of Modern Art. I put my son in a more aggressive school. I really wanted to make sure that he had a career. That he would be a good breadwinner. Turned out she was serious about her studies, too. I guess I was being old-fashioned. My daughter received a degree in biology and then became a

pharmacist. I had hoped being a wife and mother would be enough. It was enough for me. Why wasn't it enough for her?"

A pharmacist? I could see why she was so ashamed. Seriously, it was interesting to have the women so openly admit that they did treat their sons differently. When I was growing up I called my brother Jesus Christ because my mother treated him like the second coming of God (and still does).

The only time I one-upped my brother was my Bat Mitzvah. My parents were of this ridiculous mind that a Bar/Bat Mitzvah was simply about the ceremony. They had a lunch at our house after my brother's, dessert at the shul after my sister's, and well, I got a whole dinner at the shul before mine. In the mid-seventies Bat/Bar Mitzvahs were not only a popular rite of passage, they also began to take questionable taste to a whole new level. Many of the women we interviewed, however, had mixed feelings when it came to Bat Mitzvahs.

#14

What do you think of Bat Mitzvahs?

"The way I feel about all circuses—I hate them." (Mother of four, librarian, Conservative)

THERE WERE NO MIDDLE-OF-THE-ROAD RESPONSES HERE; the women either loved or hated the idea of Bat Mitzvahs. Mostly because the Bat Mitzvah is a relatively modern convention. According to the Jewish Virtual Library, the first Bat Mitzvah occurred on March 18, 1922, when twelve-year-old Judith Kaplan stepped up to the bimah of her father Rabbi Mordecai Kaplan's synagogue, the Society for the Advancement of Judaism. (Her father was also the founder of Reconstructionist Judaism.) Judith Kaplan recited the initial blessing and then read her portion of the Torah in both Hebrew and in English to the stunned congregation. After she sang the closing blessing, Judith looked up and recalled, "No thunder sounded. No lightning struck."

Most of the women were of two minds about Bat Mitzvah. Some felt very strongly that their daughter's ceremony should be celebrated as equally as their son's, while others thought they were altogether unnecessary. An elegant woman in her fifties was particularly incensed when her daughter wanted one. Part of a secular and successful group of women, she listened in on her friends' interviews, and when it came time for her own, she took off her designer jacket and toyed with her necklace. After a long sip of white wine, she began.

"When my daughter was eleven, she came home from school and said, 'I'd like to go to Hebrew school.' My husband and I fainted because we had never been observant. In fact, when I was growing up, we were the only Jews at our country club. We were about as assimilated as you can get. So when my daughter came home and said she wanted to be Bat Mitzvahed, I was mortified and I thought, Why is she doing this to us? She was to be the first person in my family to be Bat Mitzvahed. Everyone poo-pooed it, including moi, but she worked very hard. The day of her Bat Mitzvah she started singing the haftorah and everyone in my family burst into tears except me. I thought, How could this child, my child, lead us on this path? I mean, I had never been inside a synagogue until that day. But slowly,

and I mean slowly, I have realized it's a nice thing. We started going to temple, and now I go on the high holy days and it's very meaningful to me. Before then, being Jewish took up less than 1 percent of my time. I was an American. And it didn't have anything to do with our daily life. But my daughter's Bat Mitzvah changed that."

When we asked my mother this question, I got a big surprise.

"I went to Hebrew school every day for seven years. I would leave elementary school at three, run across the street at three-fifteen for an hour every day. There were thirty-three boys and one girl—me. I was the first girl to attend Hebrew School at Congregation Shaare Zedek. By the end of the year, when all the boys had been Bar Mitzvahed, they had a little service for me on Shavuot. I suppose that was the first Bat Mitzvah they ever had."

Hello? Yentl! I never knew this about my mother and it blew me away. When I told her about Judith Kaplan, she said, "Hey, I thought I was the first Bat Mitzvah."

Judith Kaplan's father, Rabbi Mordecai Kaplan, believed that religious education was important for girls because he knew that Jewish mothers were responsible for imparting Jewish values and traditions to their children. My mother was no different. She took our Hebrew school education very seriously. This did not, however, mean we had out-of-control Bar/Bat Mitvahs—quite the contrary. My brother and sister both had simple family-oriented celebrations. They each got to invite some friends over after the service at the shul. Back then I wanted my Bat Mitzvah at the Manor in South Orange, New Jersey, with the coked-up DJ spinning Captain & Tennille, the father-and-daughter dance, the scary speech by drunk Uncle Marty, and at the end, the over-the-top Venetian table—the dessert table replete with sparklers—where the kids would try to squeeze in between Aunt Esther's arm flab for a brownie. The truth is, my dream Bat Mitzvah resembled a tacky wedding.

> "It's a great way to entertain, but I think it's devoid of any meaning."
> (Mother of two, scientist, Reform)

When I turned twelve, I longed for anything that would make me seem cool. I was almost six feet tall. I was taller than not only my classmates, but also my classmates' parents and my teachers, not to mention the rabbi. My shoe size corresponded with my age. So when I was nine, I was a size nine, and when I was twelve, you guessed it: size twelve. (That was as high as it went—thank G-d!) For a while I wore boys' shoes, but they were too wide, and because I was growing so fast, I began to have all these knee and joint problems. So I had to wear special orthotics inside my shoes, and I wound up wearing old man shoes. I felt enormous, and even more unattractive than the average adolescent. I was too big for the girls' department, and in the women's department my choices were the angry housedress or a shul dress. Faced with an impossible situation, my mother dragged out her Singer sewing machine and set to work modifying the teen Butterick patterns. The only problem was that she was twenty years older than all my friends' parents and hadn't the foggiest idea about hemlines and what was considered cool. Many of the clothes she made me were au courant when Hitler invaded Poland. This gave the Mean Clique of Eight even more fodder (as if they needed it). They all lived up the hill, in fancier houses, so they literally looked down on us. For those girls there were three rites of passage. The Bat Mitzvah was the first. The second was plastic surgery—tit reduction or nose job— and the third rite was an Ivy League college.

"For my older daughters we did nothing. When my third came around, she had friends that went to an even more Orthodox school than hers, and they had special things done for them—not big fancy affairs—so I did something special for my youngest daughter.

*I made her a barbecue. Today I know Bat
Mitzvahs are accepted and I think it's
very nice."*
(Mother of three, librarian, Orthodox)

The Bat Mitzvah wars played out in the cafeteria at the
start of seventh grade. Now, every unpopular kid hates the
cafeteria, because standing there with a tray while scanning
the room for your one friend is terrifying. One day, as I stood
there scanning, the meanest of the Mean Clique of Eight
called out to me, "Hey, Judith. Can I ask you a question?"

I looked behind me, thinking there was another Judith,
as the Mean Clique of Eight usually preferred the name of
"Bigfoot" for me.

"I'm talking to you, Judith."

I mumbled something back, a little too eager.

"Are you planning on inviting me to your Bat Mitzvah,
because I'm not going to invite you to mine unless you
were planning on inviting me to yours."

"Well, yes, of course I was planning on inviting everyone
in my class."

"Oh, okay, just checking."

She rolled her eyes and went back to her friends, whispering about me, while I walked to the garbage and de-
posited my tuna sandwich. I went into the girls' bathroom,
sat on the seat, and bit my lip, willing myself not to lose it.

On the night of one of the meanest of the Mean Clique of Eight's Bat Mitzvah, which was a very fancy Saturday night gala, she arrived coming out of a cake. I noticed that every female had a long gown on; you know—the ones with the big bow in the front? I stood there in a knee-length baby doll dress with a giant bow in the back. The clique swarmed around me like bees to honey with their mean girl chorus: "Great dress." "Where did you get it?" "Your mother made it? Really, I couldn't tell." To add insult to injury, I picked up my place card and discovered that I was seated next to the kitchen door with the other nerds, as far away as possible from the Bat Mitzvah girl. That was key—how close you were to the BMG. When I got home that night, I locked myself in my room, tore off the dress, rolled it into a ball, and shoved it under my bed. I sat there in my slip and looked at myself in the mirror. Everything about me was wrong. I took the bow from the back of the dress and put it on my head. When I looked again, I bore a striking resemblance to Baby Snooks—one of Fanny Brice's most famous characters. I picked up my Goody hairbrush and sang the entire album of *Funny Girl*.

"If you're talking about a party, that's great. If you're talking about going to read the Torah and all that—I know girls can do a good or better job than men, but I am

uncomfortable with the concept because that's the way I was raised."
(Mother of three, civil servant, Conservative)

When it came time for my Bat Mitzvah, I had something to prove. I wanted a bit more than a pizza and a melting Carvel cake. Somehow I got my parents to agree to invite everyone from my class. My sister designed the invitations and hand-painted each one individually. For the goody bags, each girl got a change purse and each boy a key chain. We had plain navy blue yarmulkes made, not the really cool purple velour ones that I begged for. Henry and Ben love to wear them to *Shabbos* dinner and then look on the underside to read: "Bat Mitzvah of Judith Hannah Gold. November 14, 1975." It was the one Bat Mitzvah I attended that I enjoyed. I loved performing my haftorah and giving my speech while I stood there on the bimah behind the podium without needing a platform. For a night, the Mean Clique of Eight pretended to be my friends, and I owned that stage.

There is a saying that revenge is a dish best eaten cold. Well, years later, after a show, one of the meanest of the mean girls came up to me and said, "Hey, do you remember me?" I said, "You look familiar." (Now, of course, I remembered not only her, but every single thing she'd ever said to me.) Then she identified herself, and being the actress that

I am, I hesitated and said, "Oh, yes, right. I think I remember you now." I went to visit my mother the following day and couldn't wait to tell her the story. We were at our favorite diner, and when the check came, my mother pulled out her wallet and this little green leather coin purse. I couldn't believe it—there it was—my nerdy Bat Mitzvah present to all the girls. I shouldn't have been surprised, since my mother still keeps some of her precious jewelry in my brilliant gold-sprayed macaroni art box with six pieces of rigatoni stuck to it.

While most of the women we interviewed could accept the idea of girls having Bat Mitzvahs, when it came to the topic of female rabbis, *that* was an entirely different story.

#15

What do you think of women rabbis?

"I don't think anything is wrong with it. It just changes things. I think it's like having a strand of pearls. If you let one pearl fall off, maybe all the others will fall off."

THIS RABBI'S WIFE BROUGHT UP A GOOD POINT, AND IT got me thinking back to my adolescence. When I was thirteen, I had a sudden realization. I was sitting in synagogue watching a boy my age lift the Torah out of the ark, and I said to myself, "Fuck it, why can't I do that? This is so fucking unfair." I said it to myself, because had I said it aloud, I probably would have been struck dead by lightning. I did, however, complain to my mother, who found my rising feminist tendencies a cause for alarm. "Judith," she said, "men and women have different roles." I swore to myself that when I grew up I would join a shul where women were rabbis. When I told my mother this plan, she said, "Don't be ridiculous. There's no such thing as women rabbis." At the time, I honestly did not know if any women rabbis existed. I am sure my mother thought that if one did, her congregation was comprised of a bunch of bra-burning, men-hating "lunatics."

> *"It's fine for them to get ordained, but I want to see a man at the pulpit."*
> (Mother of three, homemaker, Conservative)

Nowadays, women rabbis are found in many Reform and Conservative synagogues. So much so that the *New York Times* recently said the rabbinate was going the way of traditional womanly professions such as teaching and nursing. We interviewed a rabbi over the phone while Kate and I were in Provincetown. When we called, we got a voice that said, "Rabbi's study." I imagined an old man with a beard poring over some forgotten text. But then a very peppy and girly voice came on. Kate turned to me and whispered, "How old is she?" So I asked her. She was thirty-seven, with two kids, and worked at a large, established synagogue on the Upper East Side. Instead of asking her the question "What do you think of female rabbis?", we asked her how she came to be one.

"When I was six I told my parents that when I grew up I was going to cut off my hair, wear a wig, and become a

rabbi. What wearing a wig had to do with becoming a rabbi, I haven't a clue. In my mind, I could be whatever I wanted. Gender was not an issue. I grew up in Great Neck, Long Island; I have four older brothers, and my father was an English teacher in high school. We belonged to a synagogue in Manhattan. In college, I majored in philosophy. I liked helping people, but I knew I didn't want to be a therapist. I played the violin, but I did not want to be a musician. I liked writing, but I did not want to be a writer. It occurred to me that I could be all these things if I became a rabbi. It was a rational solution of all those things I wanted to do. Then I lost my father in college. He had a massive heart attack. When I started applying to rabbinical school, my mother said, 'You know, your father took some courses at Hebrew Union College. Let's see if I still have any of his paperwork.' And she came across a personal statement along with his application to rabbinical school. He had never sent it in. I guess with five kids, it just wasn't realistic. By finding my father's application, I felt like he was expressing some validation. In some way the resolution of my father's death and who I am came together. In terms of being a woman and a rabbi, there is always going to be this glass ceiling because of the old boys' network. Women are going to be precluded from senior jobs, like as rabbis of large congregations. But overall it's really cool. Sometimes at funerals or weddings they do not want a woman rabbi because

some of their family members are Orthodox. And some-
times they want a woman rabbi rather than a male one. I
feel that every single day, even after eight hours of crap,
something sacred happens. This morning I officiated on the
conversion of an eight-year-old boy adopted from Russia a
month before. In the course of a morning, I can go from a
baby naming to a funeral. From moments of despair and
awareness, I find what seekers find so elusive—G-d."

Her interview got me wondering who the very first
female rabbi was. Would she be close to my mother's
definition—a humorless feminist who ran the local Hebrew
school? Since Kate is such a history buff, I gave her the as-
signment. Within the hour Kate e-mailed me back about
the first female rabbi, and I couldn't have been more
wrong. Imagine 1930s Berlin. Most of the male rabbis have
been arrested or have fled Germany, and one woman is or-
dained in secret, out of desperation. Rabbi Regina Jonas
served her congregation faithfully until she was murdered
along with her family at Auschwitz. Her existence became
known after the fall of the Berlin Wall, when a pamphlet
she wrote surfaced. In "Can Women Serve as Rabbis?" she
argued that women rabbis were consistent with Jewish law
because the laws deal almost solely with modesty. These
laws, or *Tzniut*, talk mostly about clothing and appearance,
but they also dictate how and when men and women can

touch. Physical contact between men and women was so common by the 1930s that Jonas argued the laws were obsolete.

I wish I had known about Rabbi Regina Jonas when I was growing up, because back then I did not even know women could be rabbis. I told Henry about her recently because I believe that along with inculcating Jewish values into our children, we should also convey the stories of our foremothers. I try to discuss sexism and Judaism with him in a way that makes sense. I think we're the only religion that has a prayer that men say every morning thanking God for not making them born a woman, and still every mother I know tells her daughters to marry a Jewish man. Sometimes being a woman in the Jewish religion is kind of like being a woman in comedy. I feel like I belong as much as a female rabbi headlining in Las Vegas.

#16

Why do you think Jewish mothers are the butt of so many jokes?

"Because we're funny, that's why." (Mother of six, homemaker, Orthodox)

I SUPPOSE THE FIRST PERSON I should ask is myself. My mother always says, "Without me, you'd have no act." She is constantly calling and asking me, "Where are my residuals?"

I have been lambasted for promoting Jewish stereotypes, but I've always said that they do not need any help from me. But why are Jewish mothers such an easy target? From vaudeville to the Catskills, Jewish mothers have been rebuked, reviled, and ridiculed.

"Jewish men like to deflect their anger onto their women."
(Mother of three, civil rights lawyer, culturally identified)

If you ask people who the greatest Jewish comedians of all time are, they invariably say Milton Berle, Alan King, Jerry Seinfeld, or Woody Allen. But why aren't Sophie Tucker, Joan Rivers, Totie Fields, or Molly Picon mentioned in the same breath as Henny Youngman? Did Milton Berle, Alan King, Sid Caesar, or Woody Allen really invent the stereotype of the Jewish mother? Or had it always been there, lying nascent in some shtetl, just ripe for the picking? We asked each woman what her favorite Jewish mother joke was, if she had one. Although some would profess not to know any, when pressed they all came up with at least one.

Mine has always been "How many Jewish mothers does it take to screw in a lightbulb?"

"None. I'll sit in the dark."

My mother's is "Three women are sitting on a park bench. One says, 'Oy.' Another says, 'Oy.' And the third one says, 'I thought we weren't going to talk about the kids today.'"

Although most of the women pulled a joke out of thin air, they couldn't tell it worth a dime. Whether this was some sort of passive-aggressive behavior on their part is anyone's guess. One woman's daughter wrote one out for her, "just in case" she was asked. This woman was especially nervous for some reason. A thin woman in her early sixties, she wanted to please and seemed scared that she would say the wrong thing. She clutched her pearls as she looked at me and smiled uncertainly.

"My favorite Jewish mother joke? My daughter Linda wrote this one out for me. Let me get my glasses. I haven't read it yet; I was getting the food ready for tonight. It was no trouble. Just a little something I threw together at the last minute. Did you try the salmon? Did you try the whitefish salad? Did you try the kugel? Did you try the herring? There's three kind of rugelach over there. The joke, okay— What's the difference between a Jewish mother and a vulture? A Jewish mother doesn't wait until you're dead before she eats your heart out. I wonder why Linda picked this one out for me?"

"Because Jewish mothers are ridiculous. They worry too much. They're too interfering. It's also harder for Jewish kids to shake loose from their mothers."
(Mother of two, headhunter, Reform)

Why did Jewish mother jokes arise? I always think because when you've been kicked out of as many countries as the Jews, making people laugh may get you a break. It also gave Jewish men an excuse as to why they were different from other "guys." "Hey! It's not my fault, look what my mother did to me!" Yet as hurtful and misogynist as these jokes sometimes are to women, Jewish women comedians can, and do, turn the tables. The Divine Miss M, Bette Midler, has re-claimed the lost humor of a Jewish woman comedian named Sophie Tucker. Most, if not all, Tucker's jokes are bawdy. My favorite one is "My boyfriend Ernie said, 'Soph, if you'd learn to cook, we could fire the chef.' And I said, 'Ernie, if you'd learn to fuck, we could fire the chauffeur!' " Bette Midler does a fantastic job of keeping Tucker's work alive. In many of her shows, midway through she stops singing and says, "Are you ready for stories? I have some nasty, nasty stories to tell. I've been saving them for you because I know you're going to be so delighted. These are going to warm the cockles of your tasteful little hearts. These stories come from the files of the late and great Sophie Tucker. Go ahead and applaud the old girl. She is dead, but she is not forgotten."

You have to ask why Sophie Tucker is such an inspiration for female performers? Well, she had some of that Streisand allure. Imagine, if you will, a Russian immigrant who was considered fat, and for a while the only work she could get was in blackfaced minstrel shows. But the great thing about Tucker is that she had that old-fashioned Horatio Alger fighter instinct; she worked her proverbial ass off and rose to be a great vaudeville star ranked among the likes of Fanny Brice, the heroine of *Funny Girl*. Although most of her jokes were too dirty to be recorded, they were written down for future generations of comics to admire and repeat.

I am so grateful that the Divine Miss M keeps her work alive.

What about my act? I have certainly been accused of not presenting Jewish mothers in the most positive light. I had to use my mother in my act because she was the cause of my angst. Now, just about everyone has a mother, and just about everyone's mother at times can be annoying and exasperating. This being said, I walk a careful line in terms of my comedy and my religion. I do not, for example, make fun of Jews for being frugal or so-called Jewish American Princesses. I can make fun of my mother because she's a real person, but I can't make fun of a stereotype without thinking I am doing a Cliff Notes version of the *Protocols of Zion*. (A must-read for all anti-Semites.) And in my own defense, no matter where I have performed, I have always admitted immediately on stage that I'm a Jew. I had to. When you're a comedian, your first instinct is to disarm the audience. Within the first couple of minutes I always mention that I am tall, I am gay, and I am a Jew. It's always ironic to me when I am criticized by someone who never leaves the Upper West Side (usually at Zabar's, trapped by a baby stroller). "You're Judy Gold, aren't you? I saw you at XYZ benefit [take your pick, I do a million a year] and you were talking about your mother. And I'd just like to say you're really not portraying Jewish women in a positive light." Okay, lady, you know what? You never leave the Upper

West Side and I am out there touring in Alabama doing my Jewish mother routine in front of a bunch of college kids who have never seen a Jew in their lives.

One time, when I was playing a college in Flint, Michigan, I asked the college kid who was introducing me if there were any Jews in there. She looked at me with a blank expression and then said, "Jews? Sure, we have apple juice, orange juice—what kind of juice were you looking for?" "Um, the kind that celebrates Chanukah," I wanted to scream.

Needless to say, I was nervous about doing my act that night. How would it go? But the audience surprised me. Several of the kids waited for me afterward, and one said in a dulcet twang, "Your mother is just like mine." I looked at him with his dreds, tattoos, and piercings and thought to myself, If you were my mom's kid, she'd be sitting shiva.

> "Because we're out there. We're an easy target."
> (Mother of two, literary agent, nonpracticing)

Sometimes, however, things do not go so smoothly. One night I was playing the Punchline in Marietta, Georgia. I started doing my routine and people started heckling, screaming stuff like "Jews have all the money" and "Kike." It made me physically ill, scared, and angry. I didn't want to put myself in that situation again.

After that, I couldn't go on the road for a while because I

was too shaken. A friend of mine played the same place and called me. "You know, when I first went on, I was totally freaked out because the audience was so hostile. I finally figured out by the Saturday late show that they thought I was Jewish; when I told them I wasn't, their whole attitude changed. I don't know how you do it, Judy." I do it because I love to perform.

As much as I loved my job working for Rosie, I knew that I wanted to get back to performing. But the turning point wasn't until *the* Alan King cornered me at a panel discussion we were doing at Harvard. He said to me, "Judy, you're a performer. You belong out there on stage and not writing for someone else." So I quit my job and went back on the road. It was perhaps the bravest and most foolish thing I've ever done. Why? Because I also was pregnant at the time.

Thinking back, I still have to ask, why did we decide to have a second child when Wendy had quit her job to start her own company marketing prescription drugs? I had left the only job security that I had ever really known, and the financial planner said we couldn't afford to do it. It's not like either kid was a mistake. It's not like we had one too many cosmos one night and started dialing up the sperm bank. We wanted a bigger family because we wanted Henry to have a sibling to go through life with. It was as simple as that. Plus my sister had just had a baby and I was feeling competitive.

Kate and I started interviewing our first women after I found out I was pregnant. When I began to show, we were interviewing Orthodox women. The women would congratulate me.

"You and your husband must be so excited."

"Yes," I said. "He's thrilled."

Now, I had never lied about who I was before. So why was I lying to these Orthodox women? I could tell you that I wanted them to open up to me and I thought that if they knew the truth about me, they wouldn't. That's not it. Quite simply, I lied because I thought they would judge me and not consider me a real Jew. The truth is, I came in ready to judge them in their long skirts and wigs. I hated their subservient role to men and their endless childbearing. To me, Orthodox women were something out of a Chaim Potok novel with a bit of Stephen King thrown in. But guess what happened? Of all the women we interviewed, I identified with the Orthies the most. It stunned me at first and then it made sense. They went to shul. I went to shul. They kept a kosher home; so did I. They were imparting Jewish values and education to their children, and so was I.

In fact, I agreed with them on almost everything they said, except one thing. When I asked them, "Would you sit shiva if your child married a non-Jew?", all but one said yes.

Sitting shiva is what Jews do for seven days when a family member dies. If a family were to sit shiva, they would be, in effect, declaring their child dead. I thought, Oh, my G-d, what would they do if I was their daughter? And for the first time I began to understand why it was so difficult for my mother to be open about my life to her friends.

#17

Would you sit shiva if your child married a non-Jew?

"I always thought that I would. I grew up observant, and my parents are very religious. But recently I heard from a friend that her brother married a non-Jewish girl and that she and her parents sat shiva. And after twenty-five years, she is very sorry that she did that."

THAT WASN'T THE FIRST TIME WE HEARD THAT. IN RE-sponse to this question, one of the husbands took us aside at the end of the night. He stood on the stairs of this old Victorian. He had been sitting in the dark, listening. He clicked on the light and sat down on a step. He explained that as a doctor, he had been treating various members of one family for a number of years. They were an Orthodox family and one of the sons had married a non-Jew. The family sat shiva. One day the mother came, and her appointment overlapped with the daughter-in-law she had refused to meet, and she saw the grandchildren she didn't know existed. She had no idea who they were, but she commented to this stranger how beautiful and well behaved her children were. The doctor came out of the examination room and saw this exchange. Perhaps it would have just gone unnoticed if the nurse hadn't called out, "Mrs. Steinbaum, I forgot to give you the prescription for Noah." The older Mrs. Steinbaum looked at the younger. She saw that the two children she had been admiring were her own grandchildren. The doctor said that when he called his older patient into his room, she did not speak of what had occurred, nor did he mention it. Soon afterward she switched doctors.

On the way home from this interview, Kate said, "I think that's the saddest story I've ever heard. Can you imagine, Jude, being in that waiting room and seeing your grandchildren and then not even acknowledging them? What would you do, Jude, if Henry or Ben married someone non-Jewish?" She raised the question I had never really asked myself. Wendy's mother was Jewish, so technically she was Jewish. So I had "married," if you will, within my faith. But I would not sit shiva if my child married a non-Jew. I would be upset and I would hope that my grandchildren would be raised Jewish, but I could not cut my boys out of my life because of whom they chose to love—especially after dealing with that kind of rejection for loving someone of the same sex.

"I wouldn't sit shiva if my mother died."
(Mother of two, systems analyst, nonpracticing)

In ultra-Orthodox communities as opposed to less religious communities, a family is more likely to sit shiva when a child marries outside the faith. While it is hard for a non-Jewish person to understand, one of the arguments against mixed marriage is that so many Jews died during the Holocaust that if we continue marrying non-Jewish people we are essentially creating our own genocide. That's how the whole idea of sitting shiva when a child married outside the faith came about. As one woman said to us, "I didn't survive Hitler so you could marry a goy."

"What's shiva?"
(Mother of one, publicist, nonpracticing)

But what happens when personal happiness collides with familial expectation? Oddly enough, we found our most inspiring story of family acceptance within the ultra-Orthodox community. While most said that they would sit shiva if their child married a non-Jew, a zaftig older woman in her sixties surprised us. Talking quickly in between bites of rugelach, she spoke so fast that her interview actually was half an hour.

"Would I sit shiva if my child married a non-Jew? Yes. I would. It's interesting that you ask. My eldest daughter was married for twenty-four years and had two children and a miserable marriage to not a very nice man. She waited twenty-four years to divorce him, because she didn't want to hurt us. You see the divorce is a shanda, *a disgrace. Then she met someone who was a non-Jew. It just ripped me apart. I knew, but I didn't tell my husband. I was afraid he would have another heart attack. But finally, he found out. The thing is, my daughter married a Jewish man who wasn't nice. Then she met this other man, this non-Jewish man who is wonderful; he's the best thing that ever happened to her. But we're an Orthodox family. So he converted. I never expected that. For three years, he studied everything; he had to go through the entire process— and I mean the entire process. For a grown man to have a circumcision says a lot. He's very, very, special and she's very, very happy. I think of him as a committed Jew. He doesn't know as much about our religion, but he's very caring and he loves my daughter. So you see, yes, yes, I would sit shiva if my child married a non-Jew. But she didn't."*

I admired that woman. Here she was from an ultra-Orthodox background, mired in tradition, and yet somehow she found it in her soul to accept her daughter's husband, knowing full well her daughter's happiness depended upon it. As unorthodox (pardon the pun) as her daughter's choice was, she knew that it was the best thing for her daughter. One might say that had her son-in-law not converted, she wouldn't have been so understanding. I'm sure there are some mothers out there who never would have accepted him under any circumstances. Sometimes the courage to defy convention is best exemplified by the simple act of acceptance.

A few weeks after interviewing that woman, I came home from a late-night gig and Henry had left a picture he had drawn on my pillow; it was of his two moms and him holding this baby yet to be born. I stared at the picture for a long time and I thought to myself, My son is so proud of the family we created, why am I hiding it? So I decided to be honest. Sure, it led to some awkward moments, but for the most part these women were more curious about my situation than judgmental. "So does this Wendy help? Or is she just like my Izzy, useless?"

After I told the Orthodox women, I was fearless. I started to be out as a lesbian on stage, not just at gay events. It freed me. I felt liberated. So when I finally got up the nerve to tell my own mother that I was pregnant, I thought perhaps it would go well. After all, I had gotten the Orthies on my side.

When I told her, she did that Jewish mother long sigh and said angrily, "Well, that's your business, Judith. I knew it!" Then she hung up the phone, and I didn't speak to her for two weeks, which is 154 years in Jew time (and that's being conservative). My cell phone didn't ring and I didn't call her, because I knew as soon as I called her she would start making me feel guilty. I knew exactly how that phone call would go: "Hello, who's this? . . . Oh, I didn't recognize your voice . . . How am I? Well, let's see, my blood pressure is 350 over 190, which means I should be dead. But what do you care, you're pregnant, you do whatever makes you happy and don't worry about anyone else but you, you, you, you, you. So long!"

I was angry. I did not know what to do. I wished that my father were still alive. He would have known what to do. He would have known what to say to me and to her. I felt like everything I ever said to my mother was wrong. And in those two weeks when I wasn't talking to her, I didn't laugh once. I just looked at the phone and willed it to ring. And after fourteen days, eight hours, thirty-one minutes, and fifteen seconds it did. I picked up the phone and heard "ahalloohu." I thought it was my mother because when she has her attacks, she loses her balance and slurs her words. One time she fell and was on the floor in the house overnight, and it was horrible. When I got that call, I panicked. So I yelled into the receiver, "Mom? Are you okay?!" I got another "ahalloohu." And then the line went dead. So I called back and I got her machine.

"You've reached 478-3284. I live at 310 Gibson Boulevard. On Tuesday nights from eight to ten-thirty, I go to bingo at the synagogue to help out. The money is in the top drawer of my dresser in the bedroom. The key is under the mat . . . Judith's roommate had a baby and Judith adopted him. Now Judith's having a baby. Don't ask. So long."

Now I didn't know what to do, because I was in New York and she was in New Jersey. Finally I just called the police, because I thought she'd fallen and was all alone. The police went to the house, they knocked on the door, there was no answer, so what did they do? They knocked the door down. You know where she was? It was Tuesday; she was at bingo at the synagogue. When I got to the house, there it was in the driveway—the police car. I walked into the kitchen and she was serving the police rugelach (probably frozen from thirty years ago). She was like the star of her own *Rescue 911* episode, and for her, life doesn't get any better than that. After the police left, I lost it. "This is why I am so fucked up, Ma. It's you who made me like this. I'm anxious, I can't sleep, and I'm completely paranoid that something bad is going to happen to you or the kids. Why did you make me this way? Why did I end up like you?"

My mother sighed a long sigh and then said, "So what are you going to call this one?"

"Benjamin after Wendy's mother, Bryna, and Dov after Granny."

"You give these kids such Jewish names. Watch—they'll probably end up marrying shiksas."

"You know, for a minute I actually thought you would say something positive."

My mother pushed a plate of rugelach closer to me. I picked up one, bit into it, and nearly broke my tooth.

#18

What is Jewish mother guilt?

"A man called his mother in Florida. He said to his mother, 'How are you doing?'

She said, 'Not too good. I've been very weak.'

'Why are you so weak?'

'Because I haven't eaten in thirty-eight days.'

'Why haven't you eaten in thirty-eight days?' the son asked.

His mother paused and answered, 'Because I didn't want my mouth to be filled with food when you called.'"

THIS JOKE IS AS OLD AS TIME, BUT THEN AGAIN SO IS JEW-ish guilt. In the fun and insightful collection of essays *The Modern Jewish Girl's Guide to Guilt*, editor Ruth Andrew Ellison states, "Between the ideal of who you should be, and the reality of who you are, lies guilt. And when you're Jewish, there's no shortage of people who are willing to point out just how guilty you should feel."

What is the origin of Jewish guilt? When we asked the women what Jewish mother guilt was, many professed not to know; others maintained it was something made up to discredit them. Some said it was generational. I blame Woody Allen. All during the seventies the non-Jews would watch him on film and think, What in the hell did his mother do to him? He finally tried to resolve his mother problems in the 1989 movie *New York Stories* (the segment called "Oedipus Wrecks"), where he makes his domineering, manipulative mother disappear. On *Seinfeld,* Jerry's mother is portrayed a bit more subtly, but not much. Then there's my act; if you need to know what Jewish mother guilt is, buy my CD. (Check out my website for further instructions.) Why can't Jewish mothers let go? Why is there this gut need to constantly keep their children in their control long after they are grown?

My mother took guilt to a whole new level. When I left my lunch at home by accident, I felt so guilty that I'd imagine coming home to her sobbing and shaking the bag. "Look at what you left. Do you know how hard I worked on this?" Okay, Mom, it was a peanut butter sandwich. *I'm sorry.* Every holiday, before the meal, we started with my mother's unique version of the opening *barucha*, which I renamed the "Lack of Appreciation Blessing." It was very prevalent during the Passover seders, and it went something like this: "Never again! I work so hard and no one appreciates it. Why do I continue to try? I have no idea. Well, this is it. This is the last seder you'll see from me. The last time. What's the point?" We'd look at each other and say "Amen" quickly, which would set off a sobbing jag. It was the little things that would trigger her. Being three minutes late for dinner would set her off on a cabinet-slamming frenzy, and of course, the crying. I would ask her the most mundane thing, like whether the dishes in the dishwasher were dirty, and she would get upset. I always wondered why she had such extreme reactions to such trivial things and yet wouldn't shed a tear for life's larger tragedies. Throughout my childhood, I'd look at her and I'd want to say, "Why are you this way?"

> *"A Jewish mother is chicken soup and honey cake and a little bit of guilt."*
> (Mother of three, retired, Conservative)

Now and then I examine myself as a mother (not too often, but every once in a while it's good to pretend that you're Social Services and you've just come for a little visit), and I think to myself, Do I do the same thing? I have to admit that sometimes I think I live on the Upper West Side so I won't stand out so much when I yell at the kids. I know as soon as I start, there's going to be another mother ten feet away screaming the same thing: "Why do you do this to me, why?" That's a favorite catchphrase of mine, one that has been passed down from my mother, from her mother, like a linguistic heirloom. "You're bleeding me!"—another favorite.

I remember when Ben was three, he was so bad, everything I asked him to do he did the opposite. I finally called up my mother.

"Ma, Ben is driving me crazy." There was a long sigh; my mother could barely contain her glee.

"Really. Whatever you tell him to do, does he do the opposite?"

I nearly shouted, "Yes, that's exactly it."

My mother moved in for the kill. "And afterwards does he smile?"

"Yes, yes, yes!"

I was hoping for some motherly advice; instead she said, "You were exactly the same way, Judith, enjoy your afternoon." Not only did she not give me any advice, but she made me feel guilty for my behavior thirty-six years ago.

Ben is completely not susceptible to my manipulations. I call him Teflon Ben. Nothing sticks to his conscience. When I go into my tirade, he starts maniacally smiling, as if to say, "Not going to work, Mommy." Henry, however—you look at him funny, he'll shout, "What? What did I do?" And actually I have to say, when I was kid I was like both of them—guileless and at the same time wracked with guilt.

When we started this project, Kate said to me, "I don't get this Jewish guilt thing. I mean, nobody can make you feel guilty unless you let them. I think Jewish mother guilt is just a myth." Then we interviewed my mother.

She lured Kate into the kitchen with some of her special defrosted rugulach and said, "You know, in 1972, Judith's father and I went on vacation to Israel. During the flight home the plane fell thirty thousand feet in less than one minute. I figured this was it. We're going to die. Somehow the pilot, thank G-d, regained control of the plane and he made an emergency landing in Yugoslavia. We were surrounded by tanks because we were on El Al and everyone hates the Jews, except for some reason the Dutch. Why? Maybe they still feel guilty about Anne Frank, I don't know. So we had to fly to Amsterdam with the broken plane. The pilot flew right above the Alps, nearly crashing because of the lack of oxygen on the plane. When we got to Amsterdam, and thank G-d for the Dutch by the way, I called home to say we were going to be late. I didn't explain why. Judith gets on the phone, you know what the first thing she says was? 'What did you get me?' Okay, here I almost got killed twice, and she wants to know what gift I bought her. Nice, Judith."

After this millionth retelling, I exploded. "I was nine, Mom. Nine years old. And I didn't know you almost died. It wasn't until the rabbi cornered me a week later and said, 'I heard you were almost an orphan last week, Judith' that I learned what happened. For G-d's sake, let go of it."

"You see how she talks to me, Kate? Do you talk to your mother that way, Kate? Do you?"

"No, Mrs. Gold. I wouldn't dream of speaking so disrespectfully to my mother," Kate purred like the sycophant that she is. And to set the record straight, I tripped and that's how the fork wound up in Kate's eye. On the ride home, Kate said, "Okay, Jude, there's something called Irish Catholic guilt. I grew up with that my entire life. But I tell you, Jude, this Jewish mother guilt, I've never seen anything like that before. No wonder you're all so nuts."

What was behind my mother's obsessive neurosis? Her family hadn't been affected by the Holocaust. There were no pogroms on the Upper West Side. Why did I have to write an entire itinerary with names, addresses, and phone numbers every time I left the house? Why was she the way she was? And would I turn out just like her?

#19

Do you have any stories from your mother or grandmother that you would like to share with us?

"My grandmother was born in Vilna, Poland. I tried to teach my grandma to speak and read English. I tried very hard to make out the words she was saying. One time she wrote out D-E-N-T L-E-F. (Don't laugh.)"

A RECEPTIONIST IN HER HUSBAND'S DENTAL PRACTICE told us this story at my mother's apartment and made us all laugh, and then she said very softly, "G-d how I miss my grandmother." I could understand that because I was especially close to my mother's mother, Dorothy Goldberger. She was born in 1896. She graduated from New Jersey Teacher's College and, at five-foot-seven, she loved to play basketball. (She played in high school.) My grandfather, Jesse Goldberger, died before I was born. I was named after him.

Every Friday, Granny took the bus from her apartment to our house. The bus stop was a mile away from our house, and she would walk all the way with her suitcase for her weekly sleepover. Friday through Sunday she shared my room and she showered me with attention and affection. My parents weren't the huggy, touchy-feely type, so I would get my weekly fix with Granny. She would envelop me in her arms, and I would play with her arm fat while she taught me to play gin rummy and Scrabble. Each week she begged me to read and worried about my penmanship. Having a grandmother born in the nineteenth century was really special. Her stories were incredible, and the sweetest thing about her was that each of her grandkids thought he or she was the favorite. I would write her letters from camp, and when she traveled around the world with her friends, or went on a cruise, she would always write to me. Her letters always ended the same way: "Heaps of Love, Granny."

I often think now how much support and help Granny gave my mother. My mother was diagnosed with cerebellum atrophy shortly before my father died. It's a neurological disorder, and the part of her brain that controls her balance is slowly degenerating. A side effect is dizziness, and unfortunately she spends a lot of her time in a wheelchair relying upon an aide to help her. I am so envious of my friends when their moms stay the weekend and babysit, because I'll never have that. But perhaps what I've most missed out on are the early morning talks in the kitchen. Every weekend, I woke to the sounds of coffee cups clinking and my mother's and Granny's voices. After Granny retired, she still worked as a substitute teacher, until she was eighty-three, in some of the roughest schools in Newark and Elizabeth, New Jersey. My mom finally placed her in a nursing home when she was in her late eighties. I would visit her and take her out to eat. One time, when it was just her and me, she ordered a BLT sandwich with extra bacon. Before I could say anything, she winked at me and laughingly said, "Don't tell your mother."

She died on Kol Nidre in 1987. I thought it fitting that Granny died on the holiest of Jewish holidays. It is always said that people who die on high holidays are somehow special—that they have led extraordinary lives. And in my eyes, she did.

Granny made these special Hungarian cookies called *pugochle*. She'd bake them at home, wrap them in waxed paper, and place them in a reusable metal tin. A couple times a year, I take out this stained index card that contains her recipe. Her scrawl is a bit shaky, but I know the recipe by heart. It is often said that Jewish mothers show their love by cooking the recipes that their mothers passed on to them. When I make these cookies, I hear my grandmother's laugh, I feel her arms envelop me, and I am once again the granddaughter of a truly wonderful woman.

GRANNY'S PUGOCHLE

Pinch of salt
4 cups flour
1 cup sugar
4 teaspoons baking powder
1 pound butter
2 eggs
2 tablespoons sour cream

Mix dry ingredients together. Cut in butter. Add eggs and sour cream. Mix until smooth (this requires squishing with your hands). Roll into 4 balls and sprinkle all of them with flour. Refrigerate at least 2 hours or even overnight. Roll out on well-floured board and flour the rolling pin, too. Use a glass to cut into the cookies—not too thin—about ⅛ inch. Bake in 350-degree oven for about twelve minutes. Look into the oven after ten minutes—a lot depends on how thick they are. If the dough starts sticking, keep sprinkling it with more flour.

When we asked the women about their favorite memories or stories of their mothers and grandmothers, most had, like

I did, wonderful memories of their grandmothers. One woman in her thirties broke out in her huge grin and said, "I know it's kind of morbid, but if you complimented anything of my grandmother's, she would put a piece of tape on the bottom of whatever tchotchke you had admired and write your name on it. Sometimes I would go to her house and spend the afternoon picking up her collection of candy dishes and switching the names."

Another woman, a curator who spent a long time in the art world, did not wax poetic or summon up any warm and fuzzy memories when she spoke of her own mother. Like a New York cliché, she was clad entirely in black, which accentuated her thinness even more, and spoke in clipped tones, as if she were selecting each word carefully. She would pause for effect after each sentence to make sure we were listening.

"I did not have an easy relationship with my mother. In fact I did not like her at all. I related far more to my grandmother, who would take me into the city for long weekends. My mother was cold and demanding. And yet the one thing she insisted I do with her changed my life irrevocably. When I was sixteen, she took me to hear Betty Friedan speak, right after she wrote The Feminine Mystique. *I listened to the lecture, and at the end my mother said to me, 'This is very important. A woman must have a career outside the home.'*

*I have to say up until that time, it hadn't occurred to me.
And it had a profound effect on me."*

I was happy to hear somebody admit in our interviews that she, too, had a difficult relationship with her mother. After I became pregnant, I wished that my grandmother was still alive to intercede for me with my mother. I know she would have calmed her down and talked her through it.

I worked throughout my pregnancy, and when I was six months pregnant, I got a call from the producers of *The Vagina Monologues* asking me to join the play. My mother was over the top; she hired a car service to take her from New Jersey to New York City, so she could see me perform in the Sunday matinee. The show started at three so she got there around eleven, eleven-thirty. One of my roles was that of the angry vagina. And after my six weeks in the show, I was told by the producers that I was the angriest vagina they had ever had. (And let me tell you, that's not the first time I've heard that.) But honestly, I didn't know what an angry vagina was until I gave birth.

I called my mother as my due date drew near and said, "Do you think he'll be late?" My mother said, "You were all born on your exact due dates, and your baby will be the same way." (She was controlling even in the womb.) Ben's due date was August 8, and that day at my ob-gyn's office, my water broke.

Giving birth is like being on a movie shoot. You wait around forever and then finally you get to do your scene. When Wendy handed Benjamin Dov Callahan-Gold to me, I looked at him, and I thought, Boy, that is one big nose. Luckily, his face filled out soon enough.

Ben's bris was much different from Henry's. It was bigger. Way bigger. We had it in the sanctuary of the shul. My mother came. My sister came. Sy was again the G-dfather, and his two daughters, Lizzy and Lucy, along with my sister were the G-dmothers. My mother offered to pay for Ben's bris, but I would not let her—after all, she hadn't offered to pay for Henry's. I suggested that she buy something for both of the boys. She gave me a generous check and I bought them bunk beds.

I breast-fed Ben, and he latched on and never stopped eating. We had this immediate bond. I especially loved our time in the middle of the night. I looked forward to sitting with him alone in the big chair while he nursed, and then eventually we would both fall back to sleep. We supplemented his feedings with bottles so that Wendy could bond with him as well, but he was totally on my schedule. Once I started doing stand-up again, he would wake up the minute I got home. It was as if he knew I was coming. I would feed him and we would have some snuggle time. It was my favorite time of the day.

Since we are gay parents, people often ask us the stupidest

questions. My two friends who had a daughter using an anonymous sperm donor told me that a parent at school asked them if they would be raising their daughter as a lesbian. They were flabbergasted. I told them to respond with, "Yes, exactly like our parents did. Oh, and honey, I think there's a draft, could you please put the baby's flannel shirt on, and put some socks on under those Birkenstocks? I don't want her to catch another cold. And where the heck did I put her fanny pack?" Sometimes people ask us who the "real" mother is. We act confused, and they say, "You know, the one who gave birth," and we always say we don't remember. One classmate of Henry's asked me who the "original" mother was. I wanted to say Eve. One of my favorites is when someone is really nosy and wants to find out who the sperm donor is, so they'll say, "He's just so cute. Who do you think he looks like?" I always answer, "Your husband."

One time, a very good friend asked me the Sophie's choice question: "Okay, you're in the boat and it capsizes, who do you save? You'd save Ben, wouldn't you? Wouldn't you?" I've thought about it, and I'd have to say it would depend on who was annoying me less that day, but most likely it would be Ben because Henry knows how to swim.

Although money was tight, it seemed as though finally Wendy and I had everything we had ever wanted, and I was living in this exhausted state of bliss. Then, Kate and her partner, Laurie, invited us out to their country house in East Hampton for the weekend. Their son, Timothy, was a year and a half. We sat by the pool while the kids played and Ben slept. We gossiped, did dramatic readings from the *National Enquirer,* planned some more interviews, drank stiff martinis (I had wine because I was breast-feeding) while Laurie grilled up some thick steaks, and watched *The Lawrence Welk Show* on PBS (my favorite). Along the way, we made plans for the kids and for ourselves. Henry was starting full-day kindergarten on Tuesday. Timothy followed big boy Henry around like a puppy. It was one of those magical weekends. Wendy and I talked about how lucky we were to be surrounded by such friends. We even stayed until Monday to beat the traffic. Before we drove back, Kate said, "I'll call you Tuesday to set up some more interviews."

The next morning I put Henry on the school bus for the first time by himself. It was a beautiful day, and Henry couldn't have been more excited. I went back upstairs and started nursing one-month-old Ben. At eight-fifteen, Kate called as promised. We were trying to figure out our schedule when I heard this really loud sound on the other end of the line and then an enormous bang. Did I mention Kate lives in Lower Manhattan?

"What was that?" I asked, confused. I remember it was such an odd succession of noises.

"I don't know," Kate said. "I'm looking out the window;

everyone is looking south and up. I think I should call 911. I'll call you back."

A minute later Kate called back. "Judy, I'm on the street, a plane flew into one of the towers of the World Trade Center. Put on your TV. Oh, my G-d. Judy. Another plane just—" The phone went dead. Two days ago, we were sitting by a pool fighting over *People* magazine. I turned on the news. I tried to call Kate back and I couldn't get through. When I realized what was happening, I looked at Ben and wondered what kind of world I had brought him into. I called Wendy and told her to come home. Then I went into mother mode. I had to get Henry out of school. I left Ben with Marjorie and ran across Central Park to the East Side. As I ran, the F-16s were flying above me. I looked down Third Avenue, and all I could see was smoke. And then, like in a movie, thousands of people emerged from the smoke, walking, scared, trying to get home.

When I finally got to the school, Henry saw me and gave me the dirtiest look. "I wanna take the bus home. Why can't I take the bus home?!" He was so disappointed. I didn't know what to tell him, but I knew I had to tell him something. As we walked across Central Park, I held his hand and tried to explain the situation as best I could. I used phrases like "bad guys" and "like in Israel." And then Henry looked up at me and asked, "Well, why do they hate us so much?" And I thought back to the first time I asked my mother the same question. And at that moment, it occurred to me that this is a question Jewish children have been asking their mothers since the beginning of time.

In the weeks that followed, I was like the rest of New York: stunned, bruised, scared, angry, but also really sad. That profound kind of sadness—the kind when you don't think anything is ever going to be funny again. I didn't want to work, and I certainly didn't want to continue the interviews. All I could ask was "Where was G-d?" in the midst of all this tragedy. Then Kate sent the first set of transcribed interviews, and I found my answer.

#20

What is G-d to you?

"I believe in some higher power, not a person. I believe there is somebody greater than myself. I don't see anyone up there. I don't see a face. Whenever I'm in trouble, I call on God. I say 'Oy Gutenu.' It just makes me feel better to say 'Oy Gutenu.' I say this is a big job that I'm doing and I'm calling on some kind of power." (Mother of three, teacher, Conservative)

IN JUDAISM, G-D IS AN UNUTTERABLE NAME. WHEN TRANscribing the Torah, the scribes came up with a series of names. The most important of these names is represented by a series of Hebrew letters, YHVH, pronounced Yud-Heh-Vav-Heh. In my house, G-d's name was summoned on a regular basis. My father used G-d's name with the word "damnit" attached in relation to our sprinklers that aimed every which way except the lawn, and my mother would endlessly beseech G-d to stop tormenting her. "G-d, why are you doing this to me?" was such a popular refrain that I began to believe that there was a black cloud following us in two specific areas of our lives: restaurants and cars. I knew whenever we went to a restaurant that whoever came in after us would be served before us, that when our order did arrive it would be wrong, late, and unchangeable, and lastly, if we weren't seated near the door, we would be next to the men's room, where noxious urinal fumes would force us to beg for a courtesy flush. With cars our luck wasn't any better. My parents would read every consumer report; weekends would be spent test driving, then hours would be spent evaluating every possible choice until they were sure they had the right one. Lo and behold, a block from the dealer's lot, the air-conditioning would stop working, and an ominous knocking in the engine would grow louder the farther we drove.

If my mother believed that G-d was the source of her torment, I believed that G-d was the only one who truly liked me. The few simple prayers that Granny taught me when I was four and five grew into a lifelong conversation with the master of the universe. I had always had such a strong belief in G-d, and I always believed that there was a reason for everything. That was true until September 11. For the first time, my belief in G-d was shaken, and why wouldn't it be? I found myself asking over and over again, "Why, G-d, did you let this happen?"

> *"God is the great mover. He is somebody that is all around, protects us, gives us or doesn't give us. He is the great prime number."*
> (Mother of six, teacher's aide, Orthodox)

Late one night I read over the printed transcripts that Kate had edited from our interviews, and one caught my eye. It was from a modern-Orthodox woman in her early seventies, who had gotten her law degree in her forties and still practiced, albeit part-time. When we asked her, "What is G-d to you?", she smiled an ironic smile, closed her eyes, and then spoke quickly.

"I have seven children—I had seven. My son Sam, my first-born, is no longer here with me. What was he like? Sam was very charming. He had girls all over him. But he wasn't interested in any of them. I found out about Sam when he was nineteen. He took me to a diner and told me. I was pretty calm about it. My husband is closed. He does not talk about it. Ever. My friends? I am sure they know. The rabbi knew, he must have, he visited Sam in the hospital. Everyone knows, but no one talks about it. You ask me who

G-d is and I will tell you. He is someone who is absent, but I know he is there. I do a lot of the ritual. I don't always feel a presence of G-d. Maybe one or two moments in my life. Other than that, no. That was a good son he took from me. What did my son die of? What did single young men in 1987 die of? You ask me if I would sit shiva if my child married a non-Jew? I know what my friends said, but once you sit shiva for a child, you don't ever want to do it again. I'm kind of mad at him—G-d, that is. But that's okay. Because this is my house and I'm allowed to be angry. You have to understand one thing: G-d may live here, but he doesn't pay the rent."

After I read her response, I had the sudden realization that it was okay to be confused and angry with G-d about 9/11. My faith in Him reached a new and deeper level of understanding. The next day, I called my agent and told him to start booking me again. A few weeks later I was headed to Lake Tahoe, Nevada, so Kate came with me to help me with the baby, work on the project, and do more interviews. At Newark Airport, we sat alone at the food court waiting for our flight to leave. "Isn't it eerie?" Kate said. "We're the only ones here. What's up with that?" Six weeks after September 11, travel still had not picked up.

"Security. I feel protected. God is he who has blessed me with all the greatest things of my life. Is that what you wanted to hear?"
(Mother of two, retired, Conservative)

When we got to Tahoe, we had connecting rooms. We formulated a plan: I would pass Ben off to Kate so I could sleep for three hours, then I would take him so she could sleep. Finally at 3 A.M. we gave up. I put Ben between both of us and we watched a cable access show about a trailer park zoning hearing that had a strange soothing effect on Ben and kept us bizarrely mesmerized. The next night, Kate held Ben while I performed a long set for the first time after September 11.

Equipped with a list of names, a rental car, and a map, we traveled all over Reno. We interviewed an eclectic bunch of women including a lawyer, a political activist, the wife of a druid, and a rabbi's wife. After the third one, I turned to Kate and said, "They don't talk like Jews, and they don't look like Jews either. It's so weird."

"Well, did it ever occur to you that America's Jewish population doesn't all live in THE NORTHEAST? Or Los Angeles? Not everyone sounds the same or looks the same," Kate said impatiently.

"Okay, but Kate, those accents slay me. It's not shay-bot, for G-d's sake. And listen to me, Kate, that woman we just interviewed married a druid. What in the hell is that?"

"Well, she's still a practicing Jew. So what if her husband dresses up in robes and worships Stonehenge?"

"What about the professor's husband? The Irish Jew from Dublin with the thick brogue and Guinness yarmulke?"

"Jude, everyone is different."

While Jewish women across America were different, the one thing they all shared was a sense of history—especially how cruel it had been to the Jews. It was as if they were all still protecting their children from some imminent tsuris or inevitable danger. I think that this sense of wanting to make their children feel safe and sheltered has been passed down for hundreds if not thousands of generations, but became even more pronounced after the Holocaust.

21

Were you or any of your relatives affected by the Holocaust?

"When I was a child, I had to draw a family tree for school. I asked my mom to help me. She picked up a pencil and under each of her relatives she wrote 'murdered.'"

A LESBIAN MOTHER OF TWO TOLD US THIS ONE RAINY AF-ternoon in Provincetown. She spoke quickly, confiding, "Both my brother and sister are mentally ill. I've always wondered if all the tragedy in my family's past contributed somehow to that."

Ever since I can remember, I've been obsessed with the Holocaust. How could this have happened such a short time before I was born? It was mind-boggling to me. When we interviewed survivors and children of survivors, I was always asking them how they felt, what they were thinking, and then how they made it through. I could never conceive of the emotional trauma they endured, and yet I was so fascinated by it. How did these people let go and forge ahead? As this project began to grow, we discovered that the daughters of survivors were the most eager to share their stories. Sometimes, they spoke so fast, we would have to ask them to repeat their parents' stories.

In her seminal book, *Children of Survivors*, Helen Epstein interviewed the adult children of survivors in an attempt to understand her own parents. After one particularly grueling interview, she turned off her tape recorder and wrote, "I began to cry. I typed with tears blurring my view of the paper on which I was transcribing her words and I began to remember things I had never allowed."

I had not grown up in a survivor community, so my experience with the Holocaust was limited to movies and books. When I was in Hebrew school, they started to show us films of the Holocaust on Yom HaShoah (the yearly remembrance day of the Holocaust) when we were around twelve. When they showed us the films, the Mean Clique of Eight girls would weep hysterically, and from the corner of their eyes they would look around to see if anyone was watching their histrionics. I was dumbfounded. I just could not conceive that this really happened less than twenty years before I was born.

I thought about what would happen if and when the Nazis started marching through Clark, New Jersey. Well, I had a plan in place, and it involved my best friend, Rosemary Antonelli. I had told Rosemary all about the Nazis, and Rosemary had agreed that if Hitler resurfaced (and we knew that might happen because we had seen *Boys from Brazil* three times), the Antonelli family would hide mine in the basement. I gave her a list of supplies culled from *The Diary of Anne Frank*.

For my birthday that year I asked for my own diary, and for months I would copy pages of her diary into mine, underlining particular passages that I related to. The problem was I couldn't fool myself—I mean, my vocabulary wasn't even remotely close to hers. I referred to Anne so much that my mother asked what happened to Rosemary and if I had a new best friend at school.

The truth is I really couldn't absorb that level of hatred. It all seemed so unbelievable to me. Then we met the professor. A chic woman in her seventies, she wore a brown gabardine suit with a patterned silk shirt. She looked every inch the professor of Hebrew studies that she was. She arrived with her husband, whose Irish brogue at first intrigued us, especially Kate, more than she did. However, once her husband left, and the interview began, we realized that we were talking to someone who had witnessed what I had only read about.

"I was thirteen when I got to Auschwitz. And children up to the age of thirteen were selected with their mothers for the gas chambers. I was going on that line without knowing it,

with my mother and my aunt. When we came to be selected, the officer hit me over the head with his stick and said in German—'Are you Jewish?' I said, 'Yes, of course I am Jewish, I am in Auschwitz.' He said, 'What beautiful golden hair you have.' He saw my mother; she was also blond. 'Is that your mother?' I nodded and he pointed to the left. At this point, my aunt, who was short and dark, wanted to also come along with us. The officer shoved my aunt and she fell. I became hysterical because she was my favorite aunt. I shouted after her, 'Aunt Serena, I will never see you again.' I don't know why I said that. I didn't know that within the hour she would be suffocated in the gas chambers. I was just very scared. Being with my mother helped me survive. We slept in bunk beds and one collapsed on her. She had her spine broken in two places and she wound up in the infirmary. I knew if she was in there too long, she'd be sent to the gas chamber. So I smuggled her out. I carried her around. During roll call, I propped her up. She was very weak, and during the next selection, an officer asked her, 'Can you still work?' and she wanted to say no. And I pulled on her arm hard and said, 'Say yes. Pull yourself together. Pull yourself together.' She was afraid to say no because of me, which is funny. Before the war I was a dreamer, a skinny girl who wrote poetry. And my mother was the strong, practical one. But in the camps our roles were reversed. That's why we were both able to survive."

After years of reading about Anne Frank's life, I had met someone who lived through it. We had interviewed a lot of daughters of survivors, but this was our only actual survivor.

A couple of weeks after that interview, I had a late-night gig and I started to do my Anne Frank joke and then I stopped. I censored myself, something that I am not accustomed to doing. Afterward, this woman came up to me and asked why I didn't do the Anne Frank joke. "I was waiting for it," she said. "Because of that joke, I actually went to see the Anne Frank House. I came to see your show tonight to thank you for being out." And I thought she meant about being gay, and then she said, "No. Out about being a Jew." The next morning I called my friend at the Simon Wiesenthal Center in LA, who is a child of Holocaust survivors, and I said, "Should I take the Anne Frank joke out of my act?" And he said, "Remind people what happened. I don't care how you do it." So I put the joke back in my act. Forever.

"My mother is the sole survivor of her family. She was from a wealthy family in Vilna. There was a picture taken of her family on the occasion of her mother's reunion with her sister after twenty-one years of being separated following World War I. That picture is the sole surviving artifact of two families.

Two years after that picture was taken was the last time my mother saw her mother. My mother was fifteen when she was deported to the ghetto. There were different tiers, different mind fucks I called them. One of the mind fuck experiences was those who can work will not get deported. So she worked in the railroad. At one point, it was if you're married, married people won't get deported. So a marriage was arranged for her with a boy in the ghetto. Why the adults abandoned her completely and had the marriage consummated is beyond my wildest imagination. I grew up with the sense that she really had been raped. She said she was looking for him after the war to kill him, but he was dead already. She became pregnant and she gave birth to my half-brother. When she was deported to a death camp, her son was taken away from her. If you asked me if I would be one of those people that let the child go or that went with the child, I would have gone with. She didn't because she was young and she was in shock. So her son was murdered at two."

(Mother of two, nonprofit fund-raiser, Reform)

What can you say after hearing a story like this? The fact that a person could be treated so viciously and heinously by other human beings simply because of her religion is still inconceivable no matter how many times one hears it.

In the spring we were asked to do a preview of our play that was then titled *G-d Doesn't Pay Rent Here* in Seattle at a place called the Empty Space Theatre. Nobody is more addicted to caffeine than I am, so what could be better? We thought Seattle would be like a groovy Gap ad. (I imagined everyone doing Jerome Robbins choreography, sipping grande half-skinny mocha lattes, and discussing Sartre, while living off their stock options from Microsoft.) We were excited. We packed our black turtlenecks, got ready for the caffeine jitters, and were on our way.

I felt terrible about being away from the kids for six weeks, plus Wendy really wasn't thrilled about being a single mother. Even though she was supportive of my career, she was at the end of her rope with my crazy schedule. The thing was that when I was home, I was home, and everything was fine (kind of). When I was gone, she felt overwhelmed and resentful. I think she thought I was on the road sleeping late and having a great time, while she was stuck with the kids. So in order to make it less hellish on Wendy, we planned that she would fly out after a couple of weeks and leave Henry with me. Then I would fly back on my day off and we would switch kids. The morning after

Kate and I got to Seattle, we walked to rehearsals, and instead of seeing hip literate liberals swilling coffee, we saw a lot of Kurt Cobain wannabes busking for change. We got to the rehearsal room, and the director said, "We really like the play, but we think you should take out any reference to Israel."

When we asked why, the assistant director said, "Because it's not relevant."

Not relevant? "It's the Jewish homeland," I nearly shouted.

Then we were told the people of Seattle would not appreciate us stirring up any anti-Arab sentiment. The director said, with a note of finality, "Israel has got to go."

Kate and I walked out of rehearsal, incredulous. "Do you think that this bastion of liberalism is just a myth?" I said.

"Well, Jude, I didn't want to show you this." She unfolded a newspaper and showed me an editorial. "They're blaming Israel aka the Jews for the 9/11 attacks." My heart sank. What in G-d's name had we gotten ourselves into?

22

Are you a Zionist and what do you think of the situation in Israel?

"When I turned nineteen, it was time for me to go into the army. And I did not want to go. My father was a Christian who converted when he married my mother. I figured I could use that to get out of going. So I went to my rabbi and I said, 'Why do I have to go into the army? My father wasn't Jewish. That only makes me half-Jewish.' The rabbi smiled, and he said, 'I am going to tell you a story. There was this prostitute who lay with three men one night. She became pregnant. Who was the father? No one knew. No one could, but the child was Jewish. Why? Because the mother, the prostitute, was. You are a Jew because you are born of a Jewish mother. And as a Jew you have an obligation that you must fulfill to Israel.'"

WE INTERVIEWED THIS WOMAN, A DOCTOR IN THE BA-
hamas, where I was playing a gig for an Olivia (lesbian
only) vacation. She had planned a Shabbat service and or-
ganized the kitchen to bake a challah. Before the women
left, Kate told them about the project and everyone went
around the room and shared. Not only was everyone practicing, but they were also gay women like me. Although
there were Jews from all over, there were a number of Israelis. Long after the sun had set, we spoke to them about
the deteriorating situation there.

Although I've never been to Israel, I still feel a deep
connection to it. It seems like it's the only true democracy
in the Middle East. Do I think Israel is infallible? Not at
all, but I do know that their M.O. is not blowing themselves up on buses and in crowded cafés. I do benefits for
the organization Seeds of Peace. They send Arab and Israeli kids to camp together so they can see each other as
people and develop lifelong friendships, but can I even
begin to comprehend the situation in Israel? No, honestly,
I can't.

Many of the women we interviewed had family there. My
HBO producer, Naomi Newman, set up an interview with a
woman with six kids who lived in an exclusive enclave in
New Jersey. She showed us into the library filled with over-
stuffed chintz furniture. It looked like a cross between

Laura Ashley and Mario Buatta—totally *ongepotchket*. I was a bit intimidated by her demeanor, but she quickly made us feel at home.

> *"My mother was appalled that I had so many kids, but my husband liked the whole tribal mentality. He always used to say, 'It's the Goldfarbs against the world.' My older sons went to Harvard and Yale. My daughters are headed down a similar track. However, my youngest son did not do well in high school, and I was worried about him. After he graduated, he said that he wanted to go into the Israeli army. My husband and I discussed it, and we decided to let him go. I know how precarious the situation is in Israel; I have an advanced degree from NYU in Middle Eastern studies. The problem with most Americans is that they don't know the history. They only know the sound bites they hear on TV or what the news chooses to show you. Somehow everyone has an opinion about Israel. After World War II, when there was a tremendous slaughter of Jews in the Holocaust, the British decided to give up the mandate. The United Nations voted for partition of two separate states—Israel and a state called Palestine. Who rejected it? The Palestinians rejected it. After the creation of the state of Israel, seven Arab armies ganged up and went to war with this newly created state. Even though they had overwhelming power in terms of men and material, they lost the war. In 1967 you*

get to the Six Day War. Again, Israel was victorious. Israel
ended up with tremendously more land, and they held on to
the land, thinking, Now they'll want to negotiate peace. But
again, it was rejection, rejection. Bottom line is they don't
want Israel to exist. Not now. Not ever."

Almost every woman we interviewed identified herself
as a Zionist. But I have to say my favorite response to this
question was this one: "I believe Israel belongs to the Jews,
but considering that I can't stand most Israelis, I would
never want to live there."

Now, I don't know many Israelis, but my sister ended up
marrying one. He grew up on a kibbutz, so we are from
very, very different worlds. His name is Isaac, and well, yes,
he owns a moving company. Years ago he called me and
said, "Listen, Judith, I want to get my moving truck in the
gay pride parade, what should I do, who should I call?"

I said to him, "It's so hard to get in the gay pride parade,
and by the way, you're not gay."

"Well, my staff is gay, so can you give me the number to
call?" he said in his heavily accented English. I told him
that I would look into it. A week went by, and then my sister calls me four hundred times: "Do you have the number
for Isaac? Do you have the number for Isaac? Do you have
the number for Isaac? Do you have the number for Isaac?"

So finally I called my friend who is the head of the Gay

and Lesbian Center, and she gave me the phone number. A few weeks later we were at their house having brunch, and he said, "Listen, Judith, I need to know how to decorate my truck for the gay pride parade."

I was stunned. "You're in the parade? How did you get in the parade?"

He smiled that moving man smile—you know the one—when he's got your stuff on the truck and the estimate is just an estimate. "Don't you worry about it. I got in parade. Look at this."

He picked up this gay rag and showed me an ad for his moving company. It said, "Paragon Moving and Storage." And then it had a picture of him with his shirt off and sunglasses on, and underneath it said, "Gay owned and operated."

I shouted, "This is unbelievable. You're not gay owned and operated."

"Dah—you are jealous." He grinned.

"Yeah, I am really jealous of you, I really want your life."

"Look, the people that work for me are gay. My business partner is gay, so it's the truth. And anyway, who are you to talk? You lie in your act," he countered.

"A, I don't lie in my act, and B, I'm telling jokes," I said, incredulous.

"Look, Judith, Wendy, just tell me how to decorate the truck. How would the boys like it?"

So I said in a disgusted tone, "I don't know, put disco music on it or something."

He ended up painting his truck pink with big red lips. This whole thing caused a big rift in the family because I thought he was lying about being gay owned and operated. And I was pissed off about it. So my mother called me and said, "I don't blame him, because it costs five hundred dollars to be in the parade if you're gay and two thousand dollars to be in the parade if you're not gay."

I couldn't believe that I was having this conversation again. "Ma, it's the GAY PRIDE PARADE! They're promoting gay businesses."

"He has gay employees."

"So does IBM, but they're not marching in the parade."

"Forget it, Judith. Forget it. You don't understand. So long."

So then we went over to my sister's house a few weeks later, and they had an album of pictures from the gay pride parade. All of the pictures were of Isaac in pink socks and a Speedo with oil all over his body, on his pink truck with his staff. I said to Wendy, "Make sure you drop these 'by accident' in front of my mother."

Later my sister called. "Come on, what's the big deal?"

"What's the big deal? Everyone has such a hard time accepting the fact that I'm gay, but it's okay to be gay if you can make money from it."

My sister yelled back, "That's a low blow, Judith. And anyway, his business partner is gay." I knew it was a lost cause, but I was glad to make my point.

A few weeks later, I get a call asking me if I would be interested in hosting the Gay Pride Awards. Two weeks later, I get a call from my mother. "I have a magazine here with your picture on the cover saying that you're hosting the Gay Pride Awards. The magazine is disgusting. I'm so dizzy."

Keep in mind it was a boys' magazine with lots of X-rated shots; it doesn't exactly turn me on either, but I was, like, Where the hell did she get a copy of it? It wasn't exactly at the library or Deli King.

"Ma, how did you get a copy of that?" I was so curious.

"Don't worry, Judith, I got it. I have my ways. Don't you worry about it." I harangued her until she spilled the beans. Finally, she said, "Aaron Finkel picked it up when he was walking down the street in New York. He saw it at a newsstand and said to himself, 'Hey, that looks like Judith.' And it was. So he brought me home a copy of the magazine."

Aaron Finkel is forty-nine years old and still lives at home with his parents, in the same room he grew up in. Have a nice day!

Then she went on about how nauseous she was about me being on the cover of such a ghastly magazine. So I said to her, "Why don't you turn to page seventy-four and you can look at a fabulous shot of your son in-law with his gay owned and operated business?"

"Don't start, Judith. You know my position," my mother countered.

"Ma, he's not gay. Okay? He's married to your daughter. He's the father of your grandchildren. And besides, the only reason why he wants to move the gay boys is because they're neat and they pack well." She hung up on me. I was livid.

Five minutes after I hung up, the phone rang again. It was my sister, who said, "Judith, we will see you at the Gay Pride Awards. Isaac's truck was nominated for best decorated truck."

"WHAT?!?!?!!?!?"

Okay, so that's my experience with Israelis.

In Seattle during previews, we began to notice that there weren't any Jews in the audience. Finally, I got out the phone book and called the local synagogue and invited them to the show. They were so happy that I was bringing something like this to Seattle. Every day my mother called me from New Jersey to ask, "How are the audiences, Judith?" When we started selling out, she was so over-the-top excited. For the opening, Wendy brought Henry and eight-month-old Ben. Kate's partner, Laurie, flew out with their son, Timothy. Wendy said that when she got on the plane, they tried to make her buy a separate ticket for Ben because they thought he was at least two years old. When she protested that he was only eight months old, they refused to let her board until she pulled out his birth certificate. History repeats itself.

We were so excited to have the family there for the opening. The theater arranged babysitters for us, and we had a wonderful opening night. Maybe, I thought, maybe, I would finally be able to get out of the clubs. Kate got up early and went out to get the papers. She was gone for a long time. She came back, and the moment I saw her face I knew. "Not good." I found out later she had thrown the free paper away. It was so vicious and so hateful that she did not want me see to it. "It's bad enough that I read it, Jude." She showed me the review from the *Seattle Times*. I read it and then sat silently on the filthy couch.

Later on, we took the kids to the children's museum. Holding Ben again after two weeks, and watching Timothy chase after Henry, was a comfort. But still I felt like we had failed in some fundamental way. That perhaps this dream was just that. A dream. Would I ever get out of the clubs? And how was I going to go on that night? I knew that every successful performer had been through this before, and G-d knows I'd been through way worse. Plus the audience genuinely seemed to love the show. Before I went on, Kate slipped into the dressing room. She looked at me and said, "I read all my reviews. Some writers don't. They have their agent read it to them. I read my reviews because I learn from them." I started to say something, and she cut in, "Let me finish, Jude. Look at the review in the *Seattle Times*. The reviewer wrote that she wanted to see less stand-up and more of the women. But her major complaint was that we did not explain why your mother is the way she is. Look, we're out of town. We've only been working on this for a little over a year. Let's continue working on it. This is your dream, right? Well, you've never done a one-person play before, and I've never written one. We both have a lot to learn. And I'd rather learn this lesson here than in New York."

After Kate went back to New York, I stayed to finish out the final weeks of the show. One day in my dressing room, I spied the review that Kate had tried so desperately to keep away from me. I was attacked on every level, for being a woman, for being gay, but most of all for being a Jew. The play, it seemed, was immaterial. I called Kate up and shouted, "Why is it suddenly fashionable to be anti-Semitic?"

She paused and said in her immutable mumble, "Jude, I don't think it ever went out of style." Then I remembered what my parents used to tell me, "Just remember, Judith, no matter what anyone says, everyone hates the Jews. They'll act like your friend, but the minute you leave the room, they'll call you a dirty Jew." I never wanted to believe that, but for the first time I began to believe that they were right.

23

Have you ever experienced anti-Semitism?

"When I interviewed at a major consulting firm, I was taken out to the lunch by the partner, and I said, 'Oh, by the way, I am three months pregnant and I am an Orthodox Jew.' The pregnancy, they did not have a problem with, because that's a disability that comes and goes. Orthodox Judaism is forever. He tried to convince me that consulting was not for me. I looked at him and said, 'It's never interfered with anything else. You will not know. I am better, faster, smarter than anyone else, and it will never be an issue.' And I got the job and it wasn't an issue. I have a friend who is a convert, and he said to me, 'If you think there is no anti-Semitism, think again. They smile at you and they will nod, but when the Jew walks out of the room, everyone sits and talks about the kike.'"
(Mother of three, CEO, Orthodox)

KATE TURNED TO ME AFTER THIS YOUNG WOMAN LEFT. "Boy, that kike is paranoid."

I smacked her, knocking her off the chair.

> *"I was at the student union at McGill University. There was a discussion, and I remember someone looking at me and saying, 'Too bad Hitler didn't get all of you.' I really thought at that point that this is not a person to engage with."*
>
> (Mother of two, psychologist, Modern Orthodox)

If you've never met a Jew and you're told that Jews are rich, that they control Hollywood and the media, and they have horns, well, I think you're going to have some pretty funky preconceived notions about who and what a Jewish person is or can be. I have always been up front about my Jewish identity. After all, I can't very well hide it. I do have to say that, except for that one review in Seattle, I have always chalked up my own experiences with anti-Semitism to ignorance rather than overt hatred. What would it be like, I wondered, to be called a "dirty Jew"? To feel threatened or to have my children verbally assaulted? I thought, Well, that won't happen here. Then Kate called. She was back in Utah skiing with her friends. "I just heard the most extraordinary story."

One of Kate's friends who is on the national board of the ACLU moved with her husband several years ago to a renovated miner's house in Park City. Both their married children moved within spitting distance of their parents. They have six grandchildren ages seven and under. Whenever Kate visits, she spends a significant amount of time with them. One night, she went over for dinner with her son, Timothy, expecting the usual red wine and lefty politics. Instead when she got there the mood was quiet, too quiet. The daughter-in-law was feeding her infant and told Kate:

"The most bizarre thing just happened. I was just getting the kids out of the car. And I said to David, 'Lock the doors. I don't trust the neighbors.' I said it as a funny aside because one of the neighbors was standing right there and there is really no crime in Park City. The neighbor got right in my face and said, 'Why don't you and your tribe of dirty Jews just move the fuck out of here?'

"There I was holding my six-month-old baby while this guy is going off on me. I got upstairs and told my mother-in-law, who said, rolling her eyes, 'Did you say you're not Jewish?'

"I said to her, 'My children are half-Jewish. My husband is Jewish. This is my family.' I knew her point was that this guy was so stupid, he didn't know who was Jewish and who wasn't. But nonetheless, I felt attacked by him."

Kate was silent. I thought we had been disconnected.

"No, I'm still here. I'm just watching the snow fall on the mountain. I was thinking, Jude, we hear about this kind of hate, but usually it's in the context of the past, but to have it happen now is quite stunning."

> *"A little bit in Romania when I was a child. Children calling me a dirty Jew. The last time I experienced it, I was twelve and in the States; it was from a Ukrainian girl. I nearly killed her. I nearly physically killed her."*
> (Mother of two, adult student, Reform)

What would I do if someone called my kids dirty Jews? I prayed that they never experience such attacks. I was happy that I was raising them Jewish on the Upper West Side. Here they were the norm and not the exception.

Before I knew it, Henry started first grade. Ben moved into the toddler room at day care. Wendy and I were turning into our parents. We didn't spend a lot of time alone together. Okay, we never spent any time alone together, unless the kids were asleep, and we fought constantly. We were in couples counseling. Every week, we would sit in therapy together. Wendy would cry, and I would apologize and look at my watch. I would mentally count how many more years until the kids grew up and we would be forced to spend all of our golden years together. I couldn't even imagine it. I felt great about every part of my life, but I knew we had a lot of work to do on our relationship. I did not want my kids to grow up with the constant screaming and yelling I grew up with.

Meanwhile, the political climate in the country was shifting further to the right. Pat Robertson continued to contend that gays were responsible for 9/11 and G-d was punishing America for my sexuality. As our rights were further whittled away, and more and more conservative pundits were attacking gay rights and gay marriage, another year passed. Henry started second grade, Ben moved into the big kids' room at school, and I became a Homeland Security threat. Do you like how I slipped that in? What do Judy Gold and Osama bin Laden have in common? Well, we're both really tall, we both have some facial hair, and we're both threats to Homeland Security.

It all started when I was asked to perform at this Howard Dean benefit. I wasn't a huge Howard Dean supporter, but I liked his wife, a country doctor in Vermont who wore no makeup and didn't follow him around, and did I mention she's Jewish? Plus, he was in the lead and I was so anti-Bush that I was going to support the candidate that was going to win. Also, it was a high-profile event and I'm a whore. Appearing were myself, David Cross, Janeane Garofalo, Kate Clinton, and one of the guys from *Queer Eye for the Straight*

Guy. The benefit was in Chelsea, and there were two spaces—the big donor room and the small donor room. The big donor room was filled mostly with men in Armani suits, David Schwimmer haircuts, and boxy glasses. The small donor room had a lot of women in plaid and a box of Gallo's Turning Leaf Chardonnay. Anyway, we were in the small donor room. We sat around waiting to go on, and I had a couple of Dixie cups of Char de crap, which I never do before I perform. I asked one of the guys backstage, "Can we say whatever we want?" He nodded his head like a chicken and shouted, while giving me a high five that nearly knocked me over, "Oh sure, whatever. Freedom of speech, man. FREEDOM OF SPEECH!"

I went on stage, tripped, and caught myself before I fell. There's nothing like cheap wine and adrenaline. I pulled the mic out of the stand and did my Mary Cheney joke: "Mary asks her mother if she can bring her girlfriend to the inauguration, and her mother says, 'You want your father to have another heart attack?' Actually that was my mother, playing the part of Lynne Cheney in the Lifetime movie of the week, *My Father's a Dick.*"

Everyone was laughing, and I was feeling empowered (thanks partly to the three glasses of Turning Leaf Char de shit)—and I said, "Well, thank you all for your support, and just remember, we've got to get that *living, breathing piece of shit* out of office." Now, I did not know that the press was in the room, but when I got offstage, everyone was, like, "Great, great, very funny. Very articulate." Howard Dean ran in in a rage (what a surprise), and he went on stage and said, "There's some things that were said here tonight that my campaign does not endorse."

The comics slowly edged away from him and began talking about John Kerry. The next day in the newspapers—the *New York Times,* the *New York Post,* the *Daily News*—it said that I called the president a living, breathing piece of shit, which I didn't think was any big secret, but apparently no one knew it until I said it.

It was on FOX News and CNN. There were editorials all across the country denouncing me. I started getting lots of hate e-mail. My favorite one was "*YOU FILTHY POTTY MOUTH CUNT.*" When I got one that said, "We're not responsible for what happens to your family. Sleep well," I called the FBI. They shut down my server for a couple of days. Just when I thought things couldn't get any crazier, my webmaster called to tell me my whereabouts on the Internet were being monitored by Homeland Security. Okay, here I am—no gun, no arrest record. All I have is a filthy mouth, and Osama bin Laden is walking free in Afghanistan wearing a white bathrobe and making videos, but Judy Gold's whereabouts are being monitored by Homeland Security. Then my mother called. "Judith, you're all over the news for your disgusting vocabulary. Who's going to hire you now? It took Zero Mostel ten years to land *Fiddler* after being blacklisted. Ten years! Your gigs are going to dry up. So long."

It was my mother's fifth call that day and it wasn't even 8 A.M.

24

How many times a day do you call your children?

"Three, four, five times a day. My daughters are in Israel."

How many times a day do you call your mother?

"Several times a week. I have her on retainer. She's my lawyer."

ALL OF THE WOMEN TALKED TO THEIR CHILDREN AT LEAST once a day. I think they just felt the need to connect, but I think my mother wanted to make sure I was alive. Every time I leave my apartment, my mother thinks something horrible is going to happen to me. Years ago, before cell phones, I left my apartment and went to my agent's office, and I called my mother on the phone—because it was free and I'm cheap. So we were talking, my elbow hit the phone, and we got disconnected right in the middle of the conversation. I didn't call her back right away, and I neglected to tell her that I was in my agent's office when I called. Naturally, she thought that something had happened to me and that's why I didn't call her back. When I got home, I played my answering machine. She left me this message:

"Judith, are you all right? Did you fall down? What happened? Where are you? I'm a wreck. I don't understand it. Maybe I'll call Marjorie and tell her to go over and find out what happened." Long pause. "JUDITH, WHERE ARE YOU!?!?!?" There was an even longer pause, and then she delivered the clincher. "So long."

So long? What's with the "so long" at the end of the message? She thinks Jeffrey Dahmer is chopping my body up into a million pieces and she says "so long"?

People ask me how many times a day I talk to my mother, and the answer is anywhere from one to the high double digits. After my birth, my umbilical cord was replaced with a lime green twisty cord plugged into my mother's green Princess phone from 1976. This is not to say she is a technophobe. A couple of years ago, my siblings and I bought her a computer to get her online. Every day I get an innumerable number of annoying chain e-mails. Under "subject" they contain one of those innocuous phrases like "send this to seventeen of your friends or you will be dead in three and a half hours." Because I am OCD and highly superstitious, I spend way too much time that I don't have forwarding my mother's missives in order to avoid certain death. But, for the most part, my mother relies heavily on her phone to maintain contact.

What follows are three phone calls transcribed verbatim to illustrate how utterly inane and argumentative our calls can be. (Okay, yes, I am wiretapping my mother, but I am sure it's covered under the wonderful Patriot Act that the CIA has been using to spy on everyone except the terrorists.)

CALL #1 (17TH CALL OF THE DAY, 3:45 P.M.)

Ruth: Hello.

Judith: Yeah.

Ruth: What's doing?

Judith: Nothing.

Ruth: Oh, you're talkative today.

Judith: What do you want me to say?

Ruth: Fine. I won't ask any questions. (Two-second pause.) How are the kids?

Judith: Fine.

Ruth: Henry have Hebrew school today?

Judith: Yeah. He walked alone to Hebrew school.

Ruth: I don't approve of that.

Judith: Okay, when you're here taking care of them, you can walk him to Hebrew school.

Ruth: You are so fresh, Judith. How's Ben?

Judith: Fine.

Ruth: Look, about the *Vanity Fair*.

Judith: What?

Ruth: I don't want you renewing. I have a pile here that I haven't gotten to. I'll just borrow yours when you're done with them.

Judith: FINE.

Ruth: Nice, Judith. Very nice. Well, I'm glad I could aggravate you today. It's been a delight.

Judith: Pleasure.

Ruth: So long.

(I did end up canceling her *Vanity Fair* subscription, and it seemed like every day I got a postcard from them saying, "Don't disappoint Ruth Gold." Already done. "It's not too late to make Ruth Gold happy." Oh, yes it is. Way too late.)

Then one day I forgot to call her. The next day there was a note of panic to her voice.

(1ST CALL OF THE DAY, 9:10 A.M., AFTER SCHOOL AND BUS DROP-OFF)

Ruth: Hello?

Judith: Yeah, it's me.

Ruth: What happened yesterday? I didn't hear from you.

Judith: You have a phone.

Ruth: I am not going to call and get the machine.

Judith: Why not? What else do you have to spend your money on?

Ruth: It's just remarkable.

Judith: What? What could be so remarkable?

Ruth: Right now I am so dizzy.

Judith: What did you do yesterday?

Ruth: Same thing I do every day. I was dizzy. (Whenever I introduce conflict, my mother gets dizzy.)

Judith: From what?

Ruth: Listen, the aide is leaving. Let me call you later.

Judith: Okay, thanks for depressing me. (I hate hearing about her health care attendants.)

Ruth: This is my condition. This is the way it is. (Sotto voce because the aide is in the other room.) Listen, Judith, I asked her to dust because all she does is sit on the couch all day. Then twenty minutes later, I walk into the living room and there's a huge dust ball on the floor.

Judith: Uh huh.

Ruth: Then I saw her eat a raisin.

Judith: Mom, I can't talk about this now. I have things to do. I have to go pick up the kids.

Ruth: Then I saw her blink, and she was breathing the same air as me, and she used the bathroom.

Judith: Mom, I can't listen to this anymore. All you do is complain about her.

Ruth: Well, I am thinking of writing a book. It'll be a paperback and I can write about all of the stuff that goes on here. I could call it something like *My Life with Aides*.

Judith: Great title. I'm sure that'll go right to the top of the *New York Times* best-seller list.

Ruth: Yeah, I thought you would like it. I've been saving it for you. If you put it in your act, I want residuals.

Judith: Your residual money goes right to my therapist.

Ruth: Thank G-d you have me or you'd have no act and you wouldn't be able to support your kids.

Judith: On that note . . .

Ruth: So long.

CALL #3 (9TH CALL OF THE DAY, 2:47 P.M.)

This is the "I haven't heard from you so I am going to pretend that you called so that when you do call, I will ask you if you called before and then I will subconsciously remind you that you are not calling and checking on me enough" call. (The non-Jews reading now are thinking,

What the hell is that? The Jews are like Oh, yeah,
that call.)

Ruth: Hello.

Judith: It's me.

Ruth: Did you just try and call me ten minutes ago?

Judith: No, Ma, I didn't.

Ruth: I was in the bathroom. It's remarkable.

Judith: What? What is remarkable?

Ruth: Every time I go to the bathroom, you call.

Judith: I just said that I didn't call you. (Notice now I
am introducing conflict. Check out the next sentence.)

Ruth: I'm so dizzy. (Better change the subject.) This is
the worst it's ever been.

Judith: What?

Ruth: I'm so dizzy. Am I slurring my words?

Judith: No. How long does the egg stay in the boiling
water again?

Ruth: For the fiftieth time—it's enough already. Write
it down.

Judith: Come on, you know you love it that I still need
to ask you stuff like that. Plus if I didn't, what else
would we talk about?

Ruth: So G-d damn fresh, Judith.

Judith: I had a good teacher.

Ruth: Everything is my fault.

Judith: That's correct.

Ruth: Well, I'm glad I could get your blood pressure up. It's been a pleasure.

Judith: Delight.

Ruth: So long.

I didn't call my mother about the egg recipe. I called her because I wanted to talk to her about Wendy. Wendy had been working nonstop. It seemed like she was never home, and she was constantly on the phone or checking her BlackBerry. This is someone who could never keep track of where her phone was, let alone her keys and her wallet. One night I called her because she was so late and I had to run out to do a spot. She didn't answer the phone and I got right into her voice mail. I pressed her code, and I was shocked at what I heard.

Wendy was having an affair and was planning to leave me for another woman. Yup, after twenty years and two kids, she had one foot out the door. And suddenly, all the pieces of the past couple of months fell into place. Admittedly, our relationship had been troubled and problematic for a long time. We had both gone to therapy separately and together for many years. And yet, despite all our differences, I was in this for the long haul. When I found out that she had been having an affair, I confronted Wendy. She denied it until I told her that I had proof. Her face became ashen; she looked scared and shocked, and my heart was beating out of my chest. I told her that she had to leave the apartment. Did I want her to leave? No, I wanted her to say, "It was a mistake. I love you. Please take me back."

Eventually, she did say that, and we got together for one incredibly painful weekend in Provincetown. We spent a lot of time on the beach, both of us crying, both of us trying to hold together something that had been disintegrating for so long. On Monday, she told me that it was totally and completely over.

For two months I was a crying mess. I relived every mistake that I had made, every wrong thing I had said. I could not tell the kids. I could not tell my mother. I was in a state of paralysis. Six months earlier, Rosie had asked me to go along on her inaugural R Family Vacation Cruise. We had planned on going as a family, but I figured it would be best if I went without Wendy. So the week we were on the cruise, Wendy moved her stuff out of the apartment. This way it would be less traumatic for the kids, and we decided we would tell them together the night I got home. I had told only my closest friends what was going on.

When I climbed on stage to do stand-up the second night of the cruise, I decided to be honest about the situation. I told the audience what was going on in a funny way, and then I said, "Please do not mention any of this to the kids: they don't know yet." (And they didn't.) Venting on stage was my release. Normal people process through therapy; I process with a mic and three hundred people. After nineteen and a half years, it felt horrible to sit down at a table by myself surrounded by other loving couples. I never ever thought I would be a single parent. I kept saying to myself, "This isn't really happening. It's just a bad dream. Wendy will come to her senses. She will come back to me, to us."

When we docked back in New York, I knew the inevitable would be waiting for me. Of course, with all of the discussion in our relationship, I had thought about it many times, but I never really believed it would ever happen. I kept thinking about my children and how they were never going to have that childhood I had always dreamed of for them. I dreaded the thought of them waking up in the morning in a home that wasn't mine. I wanted to be there with them every morning and every night—even if they were asleep in the other room. I'd never thought they wouldn't be with me all the time.

25

What's the hardest thing you've ever had to do as a mother?

"Divorcing the father of my children." (Mother of two, art appraiser, culturally identified)

THE HARDEST THING I EVER HAD TO do was telling my children that Wendy and I were breaking up. The night we came back from the cruise, Wendy brought over dinner and we told the boys together. We said, "We love each other very much, but we fight a lot."

Henry said, "You're getting a divorce."

Wendy said, "Yes."

And he started screaming and crying and ran over to Sy and Marjorie's. We told Ben, and he was, like, "Yeah, okay. What's for dessert?"

Wendy left and went to her new apartment. Henry came back from Sy and Marjorie's and got really upset. I sat down next to him and said, "You want to talk about it?"

And he said, "Now we can't go on the Rosie cruise next

year, because now you're just divorced and you're not gay anymore."

And I said, "Oh, that? Oh, Henry, we can still go on the cruise next year, I'm still gay. Don't you worry, I'll always be gay."

It was weeks before I could summon the nerve to tell my mother that Wendy and I had split up. I did not want to admit that I had failed at something she had never approved of in the first place. I also kept hoping, as irrational as it was, that Wendy would come back. But as we went into the first meeting with the mediator, I knew it was over. I felt like I was just going through the motions.

When our friends told their parents that they were gay or having or adopting a baby, they always used to use us as the example—you know, "just like Judy and Wendy." We were sort of considered the "normal" gay couple. The palatable ones. So for us to break up seemed inconceivable not only to me, but to all our friends as well. My heart was broken. The person with whom I had shared everything of any importance—from the deaths of our parents, friends, and relatives, to the births of our children—was gone. How was I going to survive without her?

My brother Alan called. Now, the thing you have to know about Alan is that he's the calmest person I know. He's also not very verbose or demonstrative. He's about as quiet as I am loud. He told me that he would fly to the East Coast, and that way he could be there when I told our mother. I was so grateful; for my big brother to help, it meant the world to me. He flew in from Arizona, picked up Mom, and drove her to my apartment. We ordered in kosher Thai, because for the Jews it's all about the food. After we finished eating, which took about five minutes, Alan cleared his throat and said, "Okay, now Judith has something to tell you." And I told her as calmly as I could, and yet even as I said the words, I kept hoping for a last-minute reprieve. The phone would ring, and Wendy would say, "I've changed my mind. I'm coming back. I want us to be a family again." But the phone didn't ring. I had to admit that my relationship was really over. My mother was very quiet and looked quite concerned. I didn't know what she was going to say, and then, after a long pause, the pursing of lips, and a deep sigh, the first thing out of her mouth was "Well, what about Henry? He's still going to be *my* grandson, isn't he?" In that moment, I realized how much I loved my mother.

I explained that I had adopted Henry as a second-parent adoption and that no one could take him away from her. Then I thought back to the time at his bris when I stood there alone holding Henry, wondering if my family would ever come to accept him as their own, and I realized how far she had come. And then she said, "Good." Seeing that the situation was under control, Alan left to run some errands. I started to clear the plates, and my mother cleared her throat and said, "Henry reminds me so much of Stuart."

"Ma, who's Stuart?" I said, confused. Was he a childhood friend? I had never heard her mention the name Stuart before.

She motioned for me to sit and then told me something she had never talked about my whole life. She began in a voice that was very quiet and had never been used to speak to me.

"In 1939, I was seventeen years old. We lived on Ninety-fourth and West End. It was a warm June day. I was looking through college brochures in the apartment. I opened the window. I looked out and saw my fifteen-year-old brother Stuart playing baseball. I saw the doorman come out. He grabbed Stuart's jacket and ran into the building. Stuart followed him. I went back to imagining myself as a coed. Fifteen minutes later I heard an ambulance. I looked outside. It had parked outside in front of the building. Then the phone rang. I still get an eerie feeling when the phone rings on a warm spring day. Stuart was dead. I found out later that the doorman was teasing Stuart. He was using Stuart's jacket to play keep-away with his daughter. He apparently threw Stuart's jacket to her. She threw it back to her father. Stuart reached for it, and the doorman pushed him out of the way. Stuart fell back and

slammed his head on the marble floor and died. It was one
of those random accidents that never make any sense. All
we knew was that the only son in my family was dead at
fifteen. I ripped up the college brochures. How could I
leave my parents? They were shattered. You have to understand one thing, Judith: I was waiting for him to walk
through the door and he never did. That's why I have to
talk to you children every day. I just need to know that
you're all right."

I was stunned. I thought back to my childhood—the
moodiness, the crying over nothing, the constant vigilance,
the egg timer pinned to my belt, the calling me twelve
times a day. And at that moment I knew why my mother
always says, "So long" and never "Good-bye." I also kept
thinking about her tearing up those college brochures. I
was living the life she wanted for herself, and right then, I
finally forgave her for being so crazy.

But for me it was the start of a journey. I wanted to know
more, so I went to the New York Public Library and began
to research my long-dead uncle, Stuart Goldberger. His
death had made the papers. The doorman, Herman Hecht,
was arraigned, but at the last moment before he was
booked, a doctor ran down to the precinct and said that Stuart had died from an aneurysm. Was that true? Did Hecht
know someone who called someone? Hecht was German;

my uncle was Jewish. Had that been part of the equation? It was, after all, 1939, and anti-Semitism was not limited only to Germany. But whether or not my uncle's "accident" was really intentional was a question I could not answer.

After my mother told me about Stuart, I told Kate, and she asked me to take her to the building where Stuart had died. We walked over. It was an April day cool enough for a jacket, and the sun was brilliant. In short, it was like the day he died. We stood at the entrance, and Kate said, "It's so weird, all these gargoyles, the facade, were all around when Stuart walked into the building. We're seeing what he saw."

The doorman let us walk into the vestibule. I felt such sadness. I thought about something happening to my own boys. And in that instant my eyes welled up with tears. I was sad—not for Stuart, but for my mother. People survive terrible things, but tragedy leaves an imprint. Every day now I walk around the Upper West Side, and sometimes I think, Did Stuart cross this street? Am I walking in his footprints? Are my boys playing where he played?

A month later, I went to visit his grave in Perth Amboy, New Jersey, where both sides of my parents' families are buried. How many times had we walked past his headstone with palms full of tiny stones ready to place on my grandparents' graves? How could I have missed his headstone? Well, quite simply, and sadly I might add, I didn't know he existed. When I found the headstone, I stood there frozen in time and thought about Granny, my grandfather, my mother, and my Aunt Joan standing in the same spot burying this child, not quite a man, but no longer a boy. I thought how Stuart's death affected everyone for so many years. Why was no one named after him? Why was he completely forgotten?

That August, I took the kids to Provincetown, where we have a house. I then called my mother's sister, Aunt Joan, to see if we could make a pit stop at her house in Avon, Connecticut. It's such a long ride, and this way we got to see Aunt Joan and Uncle Bernie, have a home-cooked meal, a good night's sleep, and some nice quality time with family. After dinner, I put the kids to sleep, and I went back into the kitchen. Aunt Joan was cleaning up, and when she was finished, we sat at the dinner table together. I asked her about her brother. She told me that the same year Stuart died she had come down with a terrible bout of pneumonia and she had almost died, too, but they had just discovered sulfa, a new medication, and miraculously she recovered. She told me that after Stuart's death, she felt so guilty. She felt like she was the one that was supposed to have died, not him, not her parents' only son. My grandparents closed the door to Stuart's bedroom and never opened it again. It was as though he had never existed. They ended up moving apartments because there were too many memories for them to stay where they were. Then they moved out of the building altogether, to the apartment where my parents were eventually married. My grandparents were never the same.

Provinceton was bittersweet that summer. It was the first year gay marriage was ratified by the Massachusetts Supreme Court. Weddings were performed on the beach and at the Provincetown Inn. Sitting by the pool watching the kids, I couldn't help but feel cheated. While I was wallowing in some well-deserved self-pity and wondering if anyone would ever love me again, Kate showed up with her family and insisted that we start working again. Someone once said that work cures the heart. Maybe it was Eleanor Roosevelt after she found out Franklin was having an affair. Maybe it was Golda Meir after her husband left her, or it could have been Hillary Clinton after the Monica debacle, but whoever said it was right. Work and a little something called drag karaoke healed my heart that summer.

There's a place on Commercial Street called the Governor Bradford Inn. It's the sort of place that is used as a location for *Cold Case Files*. That summer Kate, her friend Cathy, whose girlfriend had left her for another woman after fourteen years, and I spent a lot of time singing karaoke with a drag queen named Thirsty Turlington. We were on a Tuesday-through-Thursday schedule, starting at 11 P.M. Joining us was a rather motley assortment of oddballs. Most notably was a man whom Dustin Hoffman could have modeled Rain Man on. Every night he did a stirring rendition of "I'm Just a Gigolo" at the top of his lungs while rocking to and fro. There was also a morbidly obese woman dressed head to toe in tie-dye, who had a knack for singing pet songs with sexually suggestive lyrics while knocking back tequila shots. Her rendition of "Stray Cat Strut" while licking the microphone is not something I'll soon forget. Her equally large girlfriend, clad in a gauzy turquoise sheath, would angrily belt out Melissa Etheridge's "I'm the Only One" while sucking down white Russians. We found out later that they ran a karaoke school in Columbus and Rain Man was one of their star pupils. Occasionally, we would have a couple of straight drunk guys come in and scream "Money, Money." But for the most part, it was just us misfits night after night. Imagine happy hour at a group home and you'll get a good idea about how strange it all was.

Kate, being the total control freak that she is, would pick out songs, and we would toy with the lyrics to fit what happened that day. I loved singing old pop songs from the sixties, and as you can imagine, one of my favorite topics at that time was Wendy leaving me. After a couple of sea breezes and some inspired rewriting by Kate on a cocktail napkin, I launched into a rather catchy rendition of the song "Windy."

> *Who's sneaking out into her bedroom*
> *Calling her girlfriend ev'ry five minutes?*

Who's been lying to me since last March?
Everyone knows it's Wen-dy! . . .

And Wendy is gone, gone, gone.
Her new girlfriend plays golf, golf, golf.
And Wendy lies, lies, lies
Whenever I ask her who she's talking to . . .
Who she's talking tooo . . .

Who's on Celexa and Zoloft?
Who's seeing her therapist
Six times a week?
Who's taking care of the kids?
Everyone knows it's Judy.

At the end of my assault on the audience, Kate gave me the napkin where she had scrawled the lyrics. "We started this project in a bar on a napkin and now that's how we're finishing it," she said. I smiled. It had only taken us five years.

When I first began, all I wanted to prove was that I was different from the typical Jewish mother. But interviewing these women has enriched my life and my act in ways I never could have imagined. I am so grateful to all the women who invited us into their homes and into their lives. Hearing their stories gave me strength, and I also got to know my mother in a way I never had before. She's still part of my act—I mean, I have to make a living now that I have two kids to support. I need material.

So after six years of working on this project, I would like to say that I am very proud to be out—this time, as a Jewish mother.

EPILOGUE

AFTER A SOLD-OUT RUN AT THE ARS NOVA THEATER, *25 Questions for a Jewish Mother* reopened off-Broadway in the fall of 2006 for an open-ended run. After it closes, I'll tour the show across the United States.

During a talkback with the audience one night, a woman asked us who funded our interviews. It hadn't occurred to us to get funding. We went out and did the interviews ourselves. They were simple to do, and all we needed were cassette tapes and a handheld tape recorder. That's it. (In the earlier interviews, our friend Robin Kampf videotaped the women, but for the most part we kept it all as simple as possible.)

The women we interviewed provided their friends, the coffee, the lox and bagels, platters full of rugelach (or in other cases wine and cheese). We cannot thank them enough for helping us with this project. One of our goals was to heal some of the mothers who had gay children, especially those from more Conservative and Orthodox families. Should sexuality and spirituality be mutually exclusive? I hope I have shown with my life and this play that they do not have to be. It is my hope that if we can prevent one family from being destroyed by difference—whether because of a marriage outside the faith or someone being gay—then we have achieved more than we could have ever imagined. This is not to say that my mother will ever be over the moon about my being gay. It's not like she's going to brag, "Your daughter's straight; mine is not only gay, but she also has two beautiful boys with unknown donor fathers."

I would like to encourage the women reading this book to set up their own "25 Questions" coffee and rugelach party. Interview your mothers and grandmothers, ask them these questions, and record their answers. That way, in future generations, you will not have to say, "I wish you had known Zeide, she was such a . . ." You'll have Zeide's voice on tape or her image on video. Historically, it's also important to record our grandmothers. So many of our immigrant roots and stories of survival during World War II need to be known and shared, before they are gone.

Here is a list of questions to ask. Remember, you can ask them in any order of relevance. It is, however, most advisable to have coffee and rugelach on hand, as food seems to be the great Jewish truth serum.

1. What makes a Jewish mother different from a non-Jewish mother?

2. Who is your favorite famous Jewish woman?

3. Do you approve of your children's choices?

4. Would your life have taken a different turn if you hadn't had kids?

5. What's your biggest regret?

6. What's the best piece of advice your mother ever gave you?

7. Who is your favorite woman in the Bible?

8. Who did you name your children after and why?

9. How important is it for your children and/or grandchildren to be raised Jewish?

10. Are you kosher?

11. What do you think of men and women being separated at shul?

12. Do you find Judaism limiting or empowering?

13. Did you raise your sons differently from your daughters?

14. What do you think of Bat Mitzvahs?

15. What do you think of women rabbis?

16. Why do you think Jewish mothers are the butt of so many jokes?

17. Would you sit shiva if your child married a non-Jew?

18. What is Jewish mother guilt?

19. Do you have any stories from your mother or grandmother that you would like to share with us?

20. What is G-d to you?

21. Were you or any of your relatives affected by the Holocaust?

22. Are you a Zionist and what do you think of the situation in Israel?

23. Have you ever experienced anti-Semitism?

24. How many times a day do you call your children/mother?

25. What's the hardest thing you've ever had to do as a mother?